Market Dominance and Market Power

Market Dominance and Market Power

By

T.V.S. Ramamohan Rao

Cambridge Scholars Publishing

Market Dominance and Market Power

By T.V.S. Ramamohan Rao

This book first published 2020

Cambridge Scholars Publishing

Lady Stephenson Library, Newcastle upon Tyne, NE6 2PA, UK

British Library Cataloguing in Publication Data
A catalogue record for this book is available from the British Library

ISBN (10): 1-5275-5944-0
ISBN (13): 978-1-5275-5944-8

To the memory of my wife Krishnaveni

TABLE OF CONTENTS

PREFACE

> "We have all encountered moments when our mind-sets and emotions are conflicted, when our head tells us to stop and our heart tells us to keep going. It is these very conversations that … will bring clarity about (the) purpose and … direction and enable (us) to bring … clarity to (our) actions." - (Mills 2019, 12).

The prevalence of the use of non-price strategies in oligopolistic markets is by now an axiom. They seem to provide firms a degree of market dominance which translates into market power adding to that provided by the nature of product markets. However, market dominance is entirely a result of the choices of the managers of firms. Economic theory has not yet paid any attention to this concept.

The notion of market power has been around for almost a century. Two measures, the Lerner measure and the Herfindahl index have been at the forefront. Both these measures have their advantages, both in terms of conceptualization and measurement. However, they have been subjected to severe criticism and their limitations have been documented in detail. Despite their drawbacks, these measures held their ground though almost fifty other indices have been developed and utilized in one context or the other.

The fundamental realization is that while markets provide some power, as firms relate to their interface with the consumers, non-price choices have effects on market shares arising from the interaction of the firms among themselves in their efforts to capture as large a share of the market as they can even while foregoing some profits. It is necessary to integrate both the effects while constructing a measure of the market power of the industry and/or individual firms within it. This is another important development of this study.

The necessity for regulatory policy, ostensibly against monopolistic practices, has been central to reinforcing the necessity for such measurements. The use of these indices, utilized in legal debates, has been justified on economic grounds but they remain practically subjective. They are well entrenched and further debates are relatively minor.

Three aspects of these measurements have been well documented. First, these measures are computed at an industry level, irrespective of how they are defined in practice. Very few attempts at measuring them at the firm level are discernible. Second, irrespective of the level at which the measures are estimated, they are not able to pinpoint the sources, especially regarding the role of non-price strategies, of market power. The only aspects that received attention are the elasticity of demand and the mergers and acquisitions that are surmised as the sources of market dominance. Third, though the role of non-price strategies is very well acknowledged, they have not been brought into the centerfold of assessing the market dominance they provide to firms, the market power they contribute and the necessity to conceptualize antitrust relevant to some of these choices. Four reasons seem to predominate: (a) their influence, in contrast to price determination by the markets (and firms), is rather negligible (a claim not substantiated as yet), (b) the market power advantages are purely transitory in nature and they will be eliminated through competition in the markets (recent experiences do not corroborate this), (c) they offer useful information to consumers in their quest to improving their welfare (the actual choices do not seem to be limited to this alone), and that (d) regulatory policies will stifle innovation apart from inhibiting possible welfare gains (in fact, non-price strategies appear to be an innovative way of limiting the effects of the market and regulations). Be that as it may, there is little (or no) attention to the measurement and implications of market power attributable to non-price strategies of firms.

The emergence of cyberspace, importance of the services provided through the internet, and the near absence of prices that the consumers are normally expected to pay for most of the services, changed the basics of thinking significantly. The focus of the shift in the analysis centers around the use of central servers and the search algorithms by the subscribers. Two aspects of the concern are worth attention: (a) the intrusion into the privacy of individual centered information and (b) the use of advertising to generate revenues for the service providers and their implications, to the consumers, of the prices of advertised products. Clearly, that they exceed what the markets themselves can create, has been the focus of the debate. Nevertheless, the regulatory requirements around the qualitative aspects received far more attention than the quantitative dimensions.

The importance of non-price competition to the emergence of the market power of firms appears to receive emphasis in recent works. However, there is no clear conceptualization, let alone a procedure for the measurement of market power so derived. This study is an attempt to define and measure market power as it applies to the firm level as well as specific non-price strategies of firms. The important observation is that while measures at the strategy level only need to consider the interaction of the firms among themselves the others require an integration with the market determined power.

Note that various forms of regulating non-price choices of firms are already in place. Especially notable are the data mobility and number portability among mobile networks, criteria for spectrum allocation, the internet, quality standards as they relate to durable goods and regulations of electric utilities. But such regulations appear to be piecemeal and lack a welfare theoretic foundation. It is necessary to close this gap by providing an appropriate theoretical foundation.

The fundamental purpose of this work is to initiate a systematic discussion of the issues involved in this endeavor. Clearly, there is a need to develop the measures as well as specify their implications for regulatory policy. One of the major hurdles is in dealing with the multi-dimensional nature of such strategies. Information from related areas has been utilized to arrive at several, albeit tentative, procedures towards the measurement of market dominance and market power of non-price strategies. The qualitative aspects are much too diffuse and harder to examine. They will not be attempted. Several quantitative measures, based on somewhat different but related premises, have been offered. Only tentative suggestions relating to the choice of one over the others have been attempted.

It should be reiterated that some well recognized information has been utilized though suitably modified to reflect the contemporary economic scenario. Further, work of this nature necessitated utilization of knowledge from related areas. This was attempted wherever it was necessary.

I was quite alone when my wife made her way to her Heavenly abode. Srinivas and Madhuri provided me invaluable help. I greatly appreciate their concern.

I would also like to thank Dr. Adam Rummens and the entire editorial staff at Cambridge Scholars Publishing for their timely and constructive help in moving this book to its conclusion.

T.V.S. Ramamohan Rao
Kitchener, Ontario, Canada

CHAPTER 1

INTRODUCTION

> "Making sense of a constantly changing environment is less a matter of systematic analysis than of being alive to alternative ways of seeing the world; opening minds to new possibilities, abandoning long held convictions, and resisting the temptation to seek comfort in facile explanations." - (Levis, 2009, p. 354).

Abstract

The present chapter provides an overview of the activities (strategies) and objectives of firms. The concepts of market dominance and market power have been defined as well. There is also a specification of the core decision processes and their outcomes that motivate regulatory activity. Keeping these in view an outline of the rest of the chapters in the book has been developed.

1.1. Activities of the Firm

Notions regarding the firm emphasized one or more of its activities depending on the purpose of analysis. Initially the emphasis was on the production of a homogeneous output utilizing a uniform technology. Developments of technology and the advent of mass production (which signaled economies of scale and scope emphasized by Chandler (1990)) that dominated the industrial scene was the basis of some studies. Essentially, the requirement to assemble several manufactured components gave rise to the recognition of the need to supplant the market transactions to avoid what was famously called transaction costs. Given the magnitude of the number of components being assembled and the number of workers involved in production the emphasis shifted to the organization of production. Sloan's M-form organization concepts have been vastly extended by Williamson (1988, 1996, 2002) and others. All these developments emphasized only the production activities of the firm and the concomitant implications for the costs of goods produced by the firm.

Two further developments were almost simultaneous. Gurley and Shaw (1960) recognized that the largeness of production activities also meant the necessity for large amounts of capital that no one individual can offer. Hence, the importance of various forms of financing was added to the considerations of physical production activities of the firm. The other aspect that was recognized was the differences in consumer preferences for certain features that products of different firms offer. This gave rise to the notion that firms offer a variety of products that are distinct but closely substitutable. From an analytical viewpoint the emphasis all along was on the firm choosing certain products that it can produce at the lowest possible cost per unit. The firms were then expected to sell their products on markets that they could not influence in any way. It was of course recognized that the products sold on the market are differentiated. This gave rise to the notion that recognizing the value that consumers search for in products is important. At once it was acknowledged that a homogeneous market for the sale of goods was replaced by many segmented and almost distinct markets for differentiated products. The attempt was to pretend that the consumers have a clear notion of the value of the differentiated products in the market and its primary role is to arrive at a negotiated price for each of the commodities at which transactions can take place. However, given the fairly large range of differentiated products the consumers cannot be expected to have full information about all the features of differentiated products for them to make a comparison among them for the value they receive.

Firms therefore felt that they need to inform consumers of the distinctive features of their product so that they can make value maximizing choices. Even if the consumers ultimately express the value of a product to them, by specifying the price they are willing to pay, firms tend to spend some of their resources so that the consumers got to know, and can express, the true value of the product to them. The possibility that the valuation is managed by the non-price decisions of the firm cannot be overlooked.

Many products that the consumers buy are durable in nature. That is, they provide a well-defined flow of services at each point of time over a certain length of time. However, the consumer has to incur some additional cost at every point of time to ensure the integrity of the product in its delivery of the promised level of service (warranties are one of the non-price choices of the firm through which it assures the consumer of the reliability of its product). The firm may conceptually provide three types of services relating to its use at any point in time; the sale of a new durable, repair and maintenance of the durable, and products and services that constitute the result of its use at any point in time. Generally, more than one firm (a franchisee) may be involved in the delivery of each of these three services. This may be partly due to the competence or availability of resources of the firm producing the durable. It may also be due to the intention of the firm to avoid regulatory policy.

Durability of products also implies that their production requires a certain length of time. As a result, the firm develops an inventory policy to smooth the time lags between supply and demand.

Firms may also benefit from producing two or more products that are substitutable or complementary in production or consumer's choice. For, depending on the flexibility of the capital stock and the production process the firm may benefit from the economies of scale and scope they provide. Further, several products of the same brand may be of more value to the consumer instead of choosing them from different firms. Such multi-product firms achieve market dominance.

The emphasis on the concept of a firm therefore shifted from that of a production unit to one where it guides, maybe influences, what consumers buy and at what price. Non-price strategies of firms have been at the center stage for a long time. Koutsoyiannis (1982) made an early attempt to examine some of the issues involved. However, many of them are not relevant at present. There is no denying that the market dominance of each of the firms primarily results in the market shares they achieve.

Young (2012, chs.2,6 and7) brought to light several non-price aspects of the digital age and cyberspace. In particular,

> "the more we define and report on our tastes, movements, and preferences, the more targeted a market we are for advertising, and for marketing to our friends. Continually pumping out and externalizing our tastes and preferences, which is so much a part of what it is like to be a digital person right now, is just not spontaneous. It is engineered. More than that, the bias of technology, by itself, encouraged this same tendency to push data about ourselves into the world. Digital technology 'likes' itemized lists that can be moved from one context and put into another, collated with people who like the same things as we do." - (Young, 2012, 61)

For all practical purposes, private corporations, such as Google Plus, Facebook, Kindle of Amazon, and others, utilize central servers to store our 'likes' and preferences. They then utilize search engines to track potential customers of specific products and direct targeted advertising to them. This has led to their unprecedented market dominance. Though informative advertisements have been considered as enabling a customer to discover the value of a product, these new non-price decisions of firms cannot be treated as equally benign. (Of course, it can be argued that by targeting individuals directly they are reducing the costs of information they provide and thereby increase consumer welfare.)

In sum, the firm may be visualized as a series of activities that must be performed in tandem to achieve the results they desire. A single measure of the non-price choices of a firm will not be sufficient to capture the different forms of dominance they provide to firms.

1.2. Objectives and Strategies

For the sake of conceptual clarity, the objectives of a firm should be considered as statements of the features of the firm that the management wishes to achieve but cannot alter directly. The following observation is pertinent. Even if the market allows a firm to charge a higher price for the output it offers, thereby increasing its price-cost margins, the firm may not do so keeping a long run perspective in view. Instead, it may attempt to increase its market share so as not to reduce the total profits. This is the genesis of the emphasis on non-price choices. In a similar fashion, firms may choose to reduce the quality of their products, commensurate with the lower price they are charging. This is another non-price strategy. To avoid the consumer forming an impression that the firm reduced the quality of its product, it may offer warranties and/or extended warranties.

In a dynamic context, the firm may consider it prudent to maintain its market share over time. This can be achieved by striving to garner the goodwill of consumers. It can be achieved, for instance, by its advertising and selling efforts. The range of non-price choices expands. To claim that the market power of a firm is solely dependent on the elasticity of demand for its product on the market would be an aberration.

Obviously, the choices, or managerial processes, described above will be classified as strategies. As a result, it can be suggested that the objectives of the firm are a consequence of their strategies and the nature of the product market. These outcomes can be measured and reflected in the available data. However, Heath (2010) observed that

> "we can observe people's actions, but we cannot observe their motives. We don't really know what people are thinking or what they are trying to achieve." - (Heath ,2010, 31)

In other words, a statement of objectives may be necessary to appreciate the nature of the market power that firms have. Profits and market shares have been the major objectives that have been recognized. It can only be surmised that the strategies of the management result in their achievement of objectives. Econometric evidence is scanty and hard to come by.

For all practical purposes, the major emphasis on the nature of the firm has to be on the various non-price choices they make, the effect of such decisions on the value recognition, or its manipulation, from the vantage of the consumer. Consumer revelation of value of the products, as expressed in the prices they pay on the market, is no longer an axiom or exogenous to the functioning of firms in the market.

1.3. Market dominance and Market Power

To this point in the analysis the emphasis was on the production and marketing aspects of the firm. The attempt was to investigate the reasons for specific choices of firms. There have been suggestions that the consumer may benefit from the non-price strategies of firms to the extent that they help the consumer in evaluating the value of the product. In addition to signaling by firms, consumers may also independently utilize search costs to assess the value of the products they intend to buy. The possibility that the sum total of all these costs (viz., the price paid on the market, search costs incurred by the consumer and the signaling costs of the firm which will be passed on to consumers eventually) incurred by the consumer can be in excess of the value of the product to the consumer has been recognized.

Since a distinction between the strategies of a firm and its objectives was necessary it follows that firms tend to establish their dominance over rivals with respect to the choice of certain strategies. The consequences of the choice of such strategies provides the firm a market power over rivals. Clearly, market dominance with respect to certain strategies may result in increasing market power depending on the consumer interface with the firm on the market for goods. Equally, as noted above, the firm may derive advantages relative to rivals in the market. Hence, it is necessary to keep this distinction in perspective.

Of utmost importance is the recognition that traditionally economic analysis emphasized only the market power at the interface of consumers with the market and did not pay attention to its quantum derived by firms in their relation to rivals.

In sum, activities of firms, including their price and non-price strategies, result in their achieving market power. The notion can be defined as the disproportionate value of one or more objectives of a firm (that are a result of market forces and/or the actions of the firms themselves) relative to other firms. There is also a disparity between the objective of the consumer to maximize the value obtained and the profit maximization (or one of the other choices) of the firms. Such differences gave rise to the requirement of regulatory policy.

1.4. Regulation

Regulation of market power, which is a consequence of the nature of the market, has a long history. Economic analysis of regulation with respect to non-price strategies was dealt with only in a few cases. For example, quality standards. Landes and Posner (1981) and Posner (2000) objected to the regulation of non-price choices of firms on two grounds. First, they offer valuable information to the consumers when used judiciously. In practice, it has been quite difficult to ascertain whether the use of a non-price choice is merely to inform the consumer of the value of the product. Hence, that there is an excess, which works against the consumer, should be acknowledged. Second, the market power derived from non-price strategies is transitory. The functioning of markets will eliminate it over a relatively short time horizon. Recent experiences suggest that this did not materialize. If anything, firms (after obtaining information about why a consumer prefers a product) may, in the absence of regulation, be emboldened to take advantage of consumers.

The approach of the present study, to the functioning of firms and regulation in such markets, can be summed up as follows. Clearly, consumers value the products differently in a market where each of the firms is offering a differentiated product. Firms will try to assist consumers in discovering the value of the products to them. As a result, it can be expected that the threshold demand curves will materialize on the market. Every firm has the option of maximizing short run profits which result in observable price cost margins. However, firms are more likely to emphasize log run survival in such markets. Consequently, they can be expected to conceptualize a maximum market share, commensurate with the consumer valuation of its product. Even so firms try to stretch beyond this market share to gain long term advantages over rivals. The value of the product and the efficient market share, as exhibited by the consumers in their interaction with the firm in the market, will be important aspects of its market power. The primary significance of this study is in conceptualizing these thresholds. This is the basis set up in this study for the definition of the market power of a firm even if thresholds themselves cannot be measured or observed in practice. Defining the aggregate market power at the industry level will be of secondary importance.

In the final analysis, regulatory limits must consider a level playing field for each firm based on the differences in threshold values. Differences between firms persist and firms will have advantages relative to rivals based purely on the value of their products about which the consumers are convinced. This is the only practically relevant definition of efficient functioning of firms in such markets with differentiated products.

In more recent discourse qualitative aspects of market power have been considered as well. For instance, firms obtaining information about why a consumer prefers a product may also utilize that information to target non-price promotional activities to other consumers without their consent. In other words, it is claimed that there is a necessity to track the market power of a firm only if non-price strategies do not remain generic, i.e., if they are directed to specific consumers. Regulation to encompass qualitative aspects has been taken up only in a piecemeal fashion. Given the widespread influence firms have on the functioning of markets it would be worthwhile to explore this dimension further.

1.5. Sequential Approach

The following sequential approach to measuring market power and regulatory action emerges in view of the foregoing arguments. Throughout this process the modified new index of market power, amalgamating market power in relation to consumers with market power vis-a-vis rivals will be utilized.

To begin with calculate the market power of each firm. Only some firms exhibit positive market power. They should be studied further. The next step is to calculate the market power of different strategies of firms that have been identified as the signal bearers. Even in this context it will be found that only some actions need further study.

It will be acknowledged that non-price strategies have some benefits to consumers. The next stage will be to identify the quantum of a strategy that provides the necessary value information to the consumer, its observed level, though beyond this marker, that can add to the welfare of the consumers, and thereby determine whether or not the strategic action is excessive and warrants regulatory policy. Though regulatory policies should be directed to such specific cases they must be designed in such a way that they can be applied to all firms uniformly. The participants may agree to their implementation or they should be enforceable at a higher level.

The design of these concepts and procedures requires drawing information from related areas. That is, there is need for knowledge transfer as Epstein (2019, 48) expressed it. Similarly, it involves utilizing established concepts with a contemporary emphasis as Hayek (1960, 47) noted. In the ultimate analysis, irrespective of how innovative and structured these ideas are, success depends on external forces well beyond control. Hence, the credit for the success of the suggested methods should go to them.

Given the requirements of exposition this sequential approach will not necessarily be followed in the following chapters. Segments of information and measurements will be detailed wherever they are found appropriate.

1.6. Outline of the Book

This book has several fundamental contributions. Chief among them are the following. First, in markets where differentiated but substitutable products are sold it must be acknowledged that the market power of a firm arises both in relation to the consumer valuation of the product on the market as well as the market power in their interaction with rival firms. A composite market power index has been defined incorporating both these aspects. Second, it is acknowledged that only some firms in the industry will have market power and similarly, only some non-price strategies will be significant. They have been identified through an appropriate characterization of market dominance and the market power of firms and non-price strategies. In particular, the study provides a unique definition of market dominance of non-price strategies and their identification. Third, developing these indices necessitated the specification of the process by which firms identify the value of their products to the consumer while utilizing non-price strategies. This procedure resulted in isolating the mechanisms of excessive use of non-price strategies that result in the market power of firms. Fourth, the acknowledgment that profit maximization may not be the primary objective of the firms necessitated certain modifications of the market power index. Fifth, regulatory limits, instruments and their use in several contexts have been detailed. Of specific interest is the regulatory regime of internet apps.

The rest of the book is developed with this background in perspective. Chapter 2 provides the background for the Lerner measure of market power. A careful appraisal suggests that it will not be the most useful approach while considering non-price choices. The other popular measure of market power is the Herfindahl index. Chapter 3 considers it in detail and underlines the pros and cons of its use. However, its superior use, both because it emphasizes market shares rather than the maximization of profits, and the relative ease in its quantitative measurement have been highlighted. In a general sense, the market power of a firm is a result of its interaction with consumers on the market as well as its relationship with the competitors in the market. It is therefore necessary to define a measure which takes both these effects into account. This was also attempted. Chapter 4 provides the details of the classification of non-price strategies. It deals with several issues of measurement (in particular, when profit maximization may not be the objective of a firm), the amalgamation of various non-price strategies, the mixed nature of some markets where some firms are competitive and so on. The notion of market dominance and its measurement form the contents of chapter 5. The emphasis here is on the specific non-price strategies that provide each firm its market dominance. Chapter 6 then turns to the measurement of the market power of individual non-price strategies at the firm level. The channels through which market dominance results in market power are also highlighted. The important contribution of this study is in defining and identifying the firms and strategies of firms that provide dominance and market power. Chapter 7 takes up the regulatory activities in detail. This chapter also describes how the legal studies rely on the Herfindahl index in devising regulatory practices. Issues relating to apps on cyberspace have been drawing attention over the past several years. Hence, chapter 8 is devoted to a presentation of the issues involved and possible regulatory measures. It is necessary to recognize that managerial practices are not directed to merely market power but other objectives as well. In other words, market dominance will have implications for the nature of strategic choice of the management. The related details will form the subject of chapter 9. Chapter 10 provides an outline of the fundamental achievements and the requirement for future work along the lines emphasized in this study. An overall necessity for the change in emphasis to non-price strategies and its implications of the market dominance and market power they provide have been summarized. The clarion call is to use this line of analysis in further detail since that is the need of the hour.

CHAPTER 2

LERNER MEASURE

"Much of the phenomena we observe that seem organic or unique are actually the result of repeating processes and systems. By decoding the right patterns, I believe, you can achieve goals from the frivolous to the meaningful." - (Gannott, 2018, 11).

Abstract

The Lerner measure has been the most popular index of market power of industries. It represents the market power of firms in relation to consumers in the market. This chapter provides an overview of this and related measures as well as the essentials of the regulatory policies based on it. It was pointed out that profit maximization may not be the goal of all firms in imperfect product markets. Instead, it may be maximization of market share. The role of price cost margins, as a representation of the market power of firms in relation to consumers on the market, loses its significance. Other measures like the ratio of selling expenses to total costs may replace it. Further, the market power of any firm may now be related to the dominance a firm has over rival firms in the market as well. The thought process about efficient choices of non-price strategies and their role in determining market power have been indicated.

2.1. Lerner Measure

The Lerner (1934) index for measuring market power is in vogue for all practical purposes. In this method, every firm is postulated to install a large stock of capital and fixed assets compatible with the available finances and managerial processes that can be put in place to utilize the capital. When they are in place, the firm is expected to choose a level of output to maximize profits. The firm then sets the price per unit of its product so that the market is saturated. This will result in the price cost margin

L = monopoly power of the firm
= (p – MC)/p

This is the Lerner index. It can be verified that $L = 1/\eta$, where η is the elasticity of demand.

In the context of a market with differentiated products, when Cournot competition is postulated, a similar measure is proposed. In particular,

L_i = monopoly power of firm i
$= (p_i - MC_i) / p_i = 1/\eta_i$

where p_i = price per unit of output, MC_i = marginal cost and η_i is the elasticity of demand for firm i, where i =1, 2, ..., n.

Elzinga and Mills (2011) detailed several difficulties with this approach. They argue that L_i may not be a measure of market power at all. First, $p_i = MC_i$ is a social welfare maximum only if all firms in the market are homogeneous, perfect competition prevails, and production exhibits constant returns to scale. Second, firms may have monopsony power in factor markets and MC_i does not represent cost minimizing behavior. Subsequent work of Hausman and Sadak (2007), Hausman et al (2009), and Hall (2018 a,b) made attempts to correct this. A modification of the index, due to Hernan (2007), will be presented below. Third, MC is not an appropriate measure if firms incur fixed costs. In such a case $p_i = MC_i$ pricing is not feasible. The Lerner index merely reflects the need to cover fixed costs. Consequently, it does not reflect the firm's ability to increase prices beyond cost or reduction in output. Fourth, the Lerner measure is static and does not reflect any of the changes in dynamic markets where entry and exit prevail. L_i is therefore more of a measure of market imperfection rather than market power.

2.2. Related Alternatives

Boal (1995), Boal and Ransom (1997) and Hernan (2007) consider the choice of y_i as a supply side phenomenon. Note that the firm has a demand for factors of production. The gain to the firm, in choosing the resource r_i is represented by

$$\pi_i = y_i (r_i) p_i - p_r (r) r_i$$

where $p_r(r)$ = price per unit of the resource. Clearly, p_r increases with r.

Assume that firms act like Cournot rivals even in the purchase of resources. Then, maximizing π_i w.r.to r_i results in

$MRP_i - MRC_i = 0$, where MRP_i = marginal revenue product of r_i and MRC_i is the marginal resource cost of the i th input

Now, $MRP_i = p_r(1+s_r/\varepsilon)$, where $s_r = r_i/r$ = share of input used by firm i, and

$\varepsilon = (\partial p_r/\partial r)(r/p_r)$ = price elasticity of the supply of r.

Similarly, MRC = marginal resource cost = $p_r(r)(1+\varepsilon)$.

The monopoly power of the firm, revealed by its demand for the factors of production, can be written as

$$F_i = (MRP_i - p_r)/p_r$$

This corresponds to the Lerner measure on the demand side. (Surely, it is possible to develop the corresponding Herfindahl index but that will not be relevant in the present discussion.)

Hernan defines the generalized monopoly power index in the product market as

$$L_m = (p - MC)/\max(p, MRC)$$

If MRC > p the firm is paying more than it is getting back. That is, it has a disadvantage in factor markets despite its advantage in the product market. Hence, the firm has a low market power and it will be reflected in the calculation of L_m.

However, for all practical purposes, it is not meaningful to utilize this measure, despite its theoretical elegance, because Panzar and Rosse (1987) argued just the opposite. For, they assume that the firm has monopsony power in the purchase of factors of production. This then implies that the observed MC is not the minimum. In such a case the Lerner measure may indeed underestimate the market power of a firm.

From the viewpoint of empirical application, it is often acknowledged that measuring either MC or η is problematic. Hence, attempts have been made to modify it to make it amenable to easy measurement. The variant proposed by Hall (1998) is as follows. Hall defines

$L_m = p/MC$ as an equivalent measure. Note that
$L_m = (p/AC)(AC/MC) = (p/AC)(C/y)(dy/dC)$, where
y = output, C = variable cost of production, and AC = average variable cost.

Denote by $\upsilon = (dy/dC)\,(C/y)$ = elasticity of output w.r.to variable cost. Similarly, let

$$s_\pi = (R - C)/R, \text{ where } R = py$$

It follows that

$$(p/AC) = (py/C) = 1/\,(1 - s_\pi)$$

Hence, $L_m = \upsilon \,/\, (1 - s_\pi)$

However, $L_m = \eta \,/\, (\eta - 1)$ where η is the elasticity of demand. This must be recorded while interpreting it. This measure is easy to implement.

Attempts by Fischer and Kamerschen (2003) and others to account for conjectural variation of rivals made a partial but imperfect correction. Thus, despite the advantages and difficulties associated with the conceptualization and implementation of the Lerner index it was not found suitable for use in legal practice and public policy to regulate market behavior.

An altogether different point of view emerged. In imperfect product markets, where a finite number of firms sell their products, every one of them experiences a reduction in the elasticity of demand. The Lerner measure attributes the market power of a firm to this elasticity. It would be natural to examine the sources of this elasticity. It would not be sufficient to argue that consumers determine it exclusively. In effect, it is necessary to acknowledge the firm's interaction with other firms in the industry.

It is well known that it would be difficult to dislodge customer loyalty once it takes root. Loyalty of suppliers of inputs and worker loyalty also belong to this category. It is necessary to explain how customer loyalty comes about. Evidently, non-price strategies occupy that role. That loyalties of this nature affect the market power of a firm should be obvious.

It is also necessary to acknowledge that not all firms have profit maximization as the only objective. For instance, they may accept a lower price cost margin to increase their market share. Give this observation, price cost margins will have to be supplemented, or replaced, by production cost/total cost and/or selling cost/ total cost and similar measures.

A systematic generic specification of the market power of firms in relation to their customers on the market is necessary.

2.3. Regulatory Measures

An altogether different perspective on the nature of market power is instructive and practical without any prejudice to the welfare basis of the argument or the profit maximization assumption. As Landes and Posner (1981) pointed out,

> "the actual economic injury caused to society is a function of not only the deviation between price and marginal cost but also the amount of the economic activity over which the deviation occurs."- (Landes and Posner, 1981,953).

Start with the result that the output chosen under the profit maximization assumption is below the welfare maximum level. Clearly, this involves a loss in the value to the consumer from the use of the product. A change in this quantity per unit of output change can just as well be a measure of the market power. This can be stated as $L_m = .5(p_w + p_\pi)$, where p_w and p_π are the prices at the welfare and profit maximizing levels of output. Expanding p_w by Taylor's series around p_π it is obvious that

$$p_w = p_\pi (1 - 1/\eta)$$

Consequently, $L_m = p_\pi (2 - 1/\eta)$

This can be implemented empirically just as L can be. Note that C(y) does not enter the argument directly.

Deadweight loss is another possible measure. Landes and Posner (1981, 942) expressed it as

$$D = a (1 - a^{1-\eta}) - (1 - a)^{-\eta} \text{ where } a = \eta / (\eta - 1).$$

It is obvious that this measure is independent of MC calculations while maintaining the welfare basis.

In either case, the rigid mindset favoring the Lerner measure is not warranted. Incorporating changes in the position of the demand curves and the implied variations in the quantity of output sold by firms is warranted while developing an index of market power.

2.4. Role of Non-Price Strategies

Another observation is equally important. Some non-price strategies of firms; for example, reducing the cost of production by increasing the size of the fixed capital which operates through economies of scale, do in fact increase the supply in the market. However, the value of the product, to the consumer, does not change. The only implication is that a larger quantity of output is available at the same price. If firms adopt advertising and other similar measures to increase demand the original equilibrium price for any given level of output in equilibrium can be restored. The basic point should be that firms do achieve market power through such strategies, which augment their market share, though independent of changes in prices. This is the most effective way of representing the welfare implications of non-price strategies. Changes in cost matter; not the changes in the demand curves per se.

In practical reality the price charged by a firm, for any given level of output initially, may not correspond to the highest that the consumer is willing to pay when its full value is recognized. Wang et al (2019) noted the following. A customer will be satisfied with the quality of the product and the level of service rendered when the price is low. The firm may indulge in some signaling cost to inform the consumer of the higher value of the product. Let the price increase to cover the cost of the promotional exercise. The consumer will seek repeat purchases even at the higher price so long as it is less than the intrinsic value of the product. The market share is then maintained at a steady level or increases. Repeat purchases therefore imply that from the viewpoint of the consumer shifting to another product will involve a search cost exceeding the extra price paid for the repeated purchase. Not acknowledging such effects would be a disservice to the welfare economic basis advocated by the Lerner index.

2.5. Efficient Choices

Note that the above method can also offer an approach to deal with other non-price strategies; say, advertising by the firm. From the viewpoint of the consumer some search costs need to be accepted to unravel the intrinsic value of the product purchased currently and/or calibrate the potential of a close substitute in delivering the value needed. The firm, on the other hand, views its advertising as a signal to the consumer of the value of its product. The search and signaling have the effect of assessing the extent to which the product delivers the value indicated by the price charged. This will determine whether the consumer will buy the same amount of the product or the consumer will increase the quantity bought at that price. Obviously, the consumer will accept a higher price, less than or equal to the intrinsic value of the product, if the price was initially low due to lack of information.

Rao (1989, ch.5) presented the welfare efficient level of advertising in detail. Following the approach currently in vogue the demand curve can be written as

$p = p(y,A)$; $p_2 > 0$, where p_2 is the partial derivative of p w.r.to A.

In a market, where several substitutable and nearly identical varieties of the product are available, the consumer would have difficulties in identifying the correct product to buy. Some cost must be incurred in searching for the desired product. Let it be represented by $S(y, A)$; $S_1 > 0$, and $S_2 < 0$. The firm utilizes advertising to inform the consumer of its product. For low values of y it can be expected that $S(y,A) > A$ suggesting that the firm is in a better position to signal its value. Hence, there will be a value of y at which the informative role of advertising ceases. On the other hand, recognizing the need to inform the consumer about the value of its product, the firm incurs a signaling cost (with the use of A as one option) $I(A)$; $I_1 > 0$. Let A' be the level of A at which $S(y,A) + I(A)$ is minimum. It is equally important to note that there exists a value A* beyond which the consumer cannot visualize any increase in the value of the product. Surely, there is no reason why $A' = A^*$. The inefficiency in the resulting choice of y may be due to the product market conditions as well as an excessive level of advertising. It was demonstrated that this result is obtained if the ex post advertising demand curve (which appropriately represents the actual value of the product to the consumer) is utilized to define welfare. This result is in consonance with Dixit and Norman (1978). Several other results have been derived as well. For the present purpose it is important to acknowledge that the effect of advertising also consists of an increase in y chosen by the consumer. However, as before, $y_\pi < y_w$ signals a loss in value to the consumer.

Defining the Lerner measure is equally as difficult as it was earlier. However, the index based on the loss in value to the consumers would be informative. It is perhaps realistic to argue that prior to advertisements by the firm the consumer would have incurred enough search costs to obtain information about the maximum intrinsic value of the product. The equilibrium value of p, which defines the market price, both before and after the introduction of advertising, remains the same. It is plausible that the Lerner index L will be reduced while the increase in the equilibrium output level signals the source of market power that the firm derives from advertising.

It is difficult to measure the transaction costs. Hence, utilizing the Lerner measure is not possible. Instead, changes in market share are easy to trace. Consequently, the market power measures based on market share will be superior. This will be taken up in the next chapter.

2.6. Emphasis on Market Shares

It is evident from the above presentation that the Lerner measure and the entire literature associated with it recognizes price as the only parameter through which firms derive their market power. Indeed, it is taken as an immutable axiom. However, in the modern industrial context there are several other sources of market power and price determination may be the least significant at least in the context of some industries. Further, many changes have been recorded in the functioning of firms which suggests that prices are no longer determined entirely by the market. As a result, simple conceptual variations of the type described above are no longer sufficient to deal with the notion of market power of firms in the contemporary empirical setting. An altogether different perspective, based on the market shares of firms, is necessary.

To begin with, note that the notion of the value of the commodity to the user as the sole determinant of prices on the market has been questioned. Further, the idea that consumer preferences are based only on prices has been revised. Similarly, the idea that prices reflect consumer preferences has undergone a change. The reality is that firms almost exclusively determine such preferences. As Poundhouse (2010) documented extensively, price consultancy has, for all practical purposes, become a big business. Price fixation by firms has become one of their major strategies. Second, sweeping technological changes rendered dependence on market prices unreal. As Coats and Morrison (2016) pointed out,

> "for every Google and Apple there are companies like Kodak, a former industrial giant crushed by digital technology, and Hewlett-Packard, a long time star fallen on bad times". – (Coats and Morrison, 2016,147).

Third, many products in the market have long life and consumers value services from them at any point of time. Is it necessary to look at the market prices for the purchase of such products or the prices for servicing and flow of services? Fourth, industries like telecommunications, the internet and airlines are not free markets but, instead, they are strictly regulated. Fifth, some activities such as telephones and mobile spectrum involve large costs and thereby experience some market power. For some products that are in short supply, or, where their supply is fixed the process of auctions has taken root. Sixth, companies like Google and Facebook do not charge any price to their customers directly. Instead, they obtain their revenues from advertising. Similarly, firms in the hotel and hospitality industries charge much more by claiming that they match customers with their needs since they have extensive data on individual needs, the supplier profiles and the search engines to match the finer details. Indeed, as Beattie (2009) pointed out, companies strive for

> “more efficient ways of operating, for a smarter way to price their products - anything that will win them more customers and give them an edge over competition.” - (Beattie, 2009, 10)

It is therefore possible to argue that in a market where a number of firms are offering nearly close substitutes the consumer is really not bothered if one or more firms are not offering the theoretically defined welfare maximizing prices and levels of output. They can readily switch between products if they are not satisfied with one or the other.

2.7. In Perspective

A significant aspect of the behavior of firms characterized as differentiated oligopoly can be inferred by paraphrasing Hicks (1935, p.8). In non-competitive environments, where firms experience sharply rising subjective costs, they are more likely to utilize their advantage much more by not bothering to choose strategies that are near the choice of rivals. Instead, they design their own strategies to move towards the maximum possible market power to themselves. Only some strategies, out of several available choices, would be relevant given the objectives of the firm. Non-price strategies have a more important role in determining the market power of firms.

The most important conclusions from this chapter are as follows. First, the Lerner measure is difficult to estimate and it is sensitive to the estimated values of the parameters. As a result, it has not been used in regulatory practices. Second, non-price strategies are ubiquitous. Their effect on the market power is through increases in market share rather than L. It is essential that the analysis is directed to reflect this empirical reality.

CHAPTER 3

HERFINDAHL INDEX

> "It rarely pays to argue that any human being is incapable of weighing the pros and cons of the decision in front of him. They are less likely to make mistakes when doing something familiar which is a point in favor of rational choice theory." - (Harford, 2002, 18)

Abstract

The other commonly used measure of market power is the Herfindahl index based on market shares. However, there have been reports of various shortcomings of this index. More specifically, it was claimed that there is no welfare theoretic basis for it. It was shown that this is not true. The Linda index and several other variations have been outlined. A new index based on the effects of the interaction of a firm with the consumers in the market as well as its interaction with the rival firms is presented. A preference for this index over the Lerner measure is also indicated.

3.1. The Definition

As noted earlier, the Herfindhal index is another popular measure of market power. The construction of the index is based on the market shares of each of the firms in the market. To start the analysis, assume that each of the firms in the market produces only one product. Let S_i be the sales revenue of firm i; i = 1, 2, ..., n. Define

S = total sales in the market = $\sum S_i$, where the summation is over 1 through n, and
$s_i = S_i/S$ = market share of the firm i

The Herfindahl index of concentration is defined as

$H = \sum s_i^2$ where the sum is over i

Note the following. Suppose $s_1 = 1$ and $s_i = 0$ for all other i. Then, H = 1 and indicates that there is only one firm in the market. Assume, on the other hand, $s_i = 1/n$ for all i. In such a case $H = 1/n$. Based on this logic $n = 1/H$ is generally designated as the number of firms with an equal market share in the market. (As will be noted later, while constructing regulatory measures this is usually the accepted definition of a competitive market.)

It was noted earlier that the measurement of marginal cost has been difficult while constructing the Lerner index. By way of contrast, the H index is much easier to compute since it does not require the measurement of marginal cost. Even so, several difficulties with the use of H have been noted.

3.2. Difficulties with the Index

Consider the measurement problem to begin with. First, Scherer (1990, 73) argued that the use of a quadratic term s^2 cannot be justified on economic grounds. Much earlier, Simpson (1949) provided a proximate answer. Let S denote the total market sales. Consider choosing two units from S. The number of ways of choosing this is S(S-1). Now, assume that the sales of firm i can be written as S_i. The number of ways in which the two items are drawn from firm i will be $S_i(S_i - 1)$. Hence, the probability of $s_i = S_i/S$ can be represented by

$$p = S_i(S_i - 1)/ S(S - 1)$$

p can be approximated by s_i^2 if both S_i and S are sufficiently large. To be sure, even from a statistical viewpoint, there is no reason why the draw of two items should be considered. On the other hand, Dansby and Willig (1979) interpreted the square terms as a representation of the Eucledian distance between the s_i s. It is more pertinent to note that no specific economic reason has been offered. Second, Hall and Tideman (1967, 164) noted that assigning equal weights to all s_i cannot be justified when dealing with differentiated products. However, there is no appropriate economic theory to conceptualize an alternative.

Hanna and Kay (1971) postulated

$$HK = (\sum \alpha_i s_i^{\rho})^{-\sigma}, \text{ where } \sigma = 1/(1-\rho)$$

taking a variety of substitution possibilities into account. HK reduces to the Herfindal index if $\alpha_i = 1$ for all i and $\rho = 2$. Clearly, the values of ρ and α_i will be estimated from the data rather than postulate values for them. Nonetheless this approach does not offer an adequate theoretical reason for its choice. (Observe that α_i can be made to depend on the Lerner measure thereby capturing the market power of the firm attributable to its interaction with the consumers on the market. This will be utilized in the new index constructed in section 3.6 below.) A different approach was suggested by Liejesen (2004). To begin with a source of substitution among s_i's has been identified. For instance, in the context of a flight between two destinations a passenger has two choices: either to choose a direct flight or another one involving two or more intermediate stops. Clearly, each of these choices implies a different time taken and have different prices. An index can be constructed to represent the substitution and s_i weighted accordingly. Many similar alternatives have been attempted but it would be fair to say that the basic issue is not resolved. There was always a lurking question as to why cost considerations do not have any role in constructing H.

Syverson (2019) summarized many other conceptual problems. First, H does not represent the functioning of a market. Instead, it captures the outcome of the functioning of the market. (Note that the price and the quantity bought are determined simultaneously. This argument is flimsy.) Hence, it cannot identify the core determinants of competitiveness in the market. Similarly,

> "concentration is about relative revenue and thus includes no information about costs or profits." -(Syverson,2019 ,25).

(Even here it must be noted that the markets determine the price and output concomitantly.) Second, in a market where firms sell differentiated but substitutable products, with heightened differences in size and costs of production, larger firms take advantage of their lower costs due to economies of scale and experience higher market shares. They can afford to operate with lower price-cost margins while the concentration reflected in the H index increases. (This, indeed, is a source of market power. Adhering to price cost margins as the only measure is unwarranted.) Similarly, in monopolistic markets, where the profit of a firm is near zero, each of the firms has a significant market power (based on the lower elasticity of demand) even if the market share of each of them is low.

Another major difficulty with H can be explained by conceptualizing the relationship between H and L. Assume, now, that the market for the products of firms, even if they are differentiated, have a single market in which the price set by the market can be represented by

$$p = p(y,) \text{ where } y = \sum y_i$$

where, as before, the summation is over $i = 1, 2, ..., n$.

The profit for firm i can now be represented by

$\pi_i = p(y)y_i - C_i\ (y_i)$, where
$C_i(y_i)$ = the cost of producing y_i.

The conventional profit maximizing assumption then results in

$p(y) + y_i\, p_1(y) = MC_i\ (y_i)$, where $p_1 = dp/dy$ and MC_i is the marginal cost of firm i.

This characterization makes the Cournot assumption that all other firms hold their y_i constant.

Hence,

$p(y) - MC_i(y_i) = y_i\, dp(y)/dy$
Consequently, $L_i = [p(y) - MC_i]/p(y) = s_i/\ \eta$, where $s_i = y_i/y$

Define

L = The Lerner measure = $\sum s_i\ [p(y) - MC_i]/p = \sum s_i^2/\eta = H/\eta$

This establishes a relationship between L and H. (Observe that, given the same η for all the firms, the differences in s_i must be due to the differences in the cost of production. Hence, any index based on s_i acknowledges the role of costs of production in providing any firm the market dominance that it has.)

Observe that in the context of differentiated oligopoly with Cournot rivals the demand curve for firm i will be $p_i = p_i\ (y_i)$ so that the profit for firm i is

$\pi_i = p_i(y_i)\ y_i - C_i(yi)$

and profit maximization results in

$L_i = (p_i - MC_i)/p_i = 1/\eta_i$

(Intuitively when this measure is used for calculating the market power index it must be acknowledged that only a fraction s_i of L_i will carry over to the firm. This has not been generally acknowledged. The following index therefore misses an important aspect of the characterization of the industry level market power. As will be evident from section 3.6 this is the fundamental change brought about in defining the new index.)

Consequently, the market power in the industry will be

$$L = \sum s_i L_i = \sum s_i/\eta_i$$

Define

$$H_m = \sum s_i^2/\eta_i^2$$

analogous to the Herfindahl index. Observe that L and H_m move in tandem with different values of η_i. This eliminates the possibility of a negative relationship between L and H_m that Syverson (2019) emphasized.

The assumption that η is a constant for all firms is crucial. However, when the market consists of firms offering differentiated products the elasticity will be different for each of them. As Syverson (2019) documented, the elasticity of demand will be larger when there is a high degree of substitution among products. This reduces price cost margins, makes it easier for low cost large firms (due to economies of scale) to dominate and thereby increase H. The other bothersome aspect is the local de-concentration of markets. For, many large conglomerates create geographically separated subsidiaries thereby reducing local concentration even when they have significant market power at the global level. This calls for an appropriate definition of the market for the firm's products. Further studies by Boal (1995), Boal and Ransom (1997) and Hernan (2007) considered the monopolistic nature of factor markets.

However, several issues remain. Syverson (2019) therefore believes that an index of concentration, such as H, is worse than a measure of market power unless a positive relationship between L and H can be established. This argument is not entirely convincing unless there is an aprioi judgment in favor of the Lerner index. For, in the context of differentiated oligopoly the relationship between L and H is not documented.

One further observation is in order. The differences in the market demand for products is at the apex of determining the market shares of firms. In a similar vein, the firms experiencing lower costs will elicit a higher market share (to be sure, Syverson (2019) and others also acknowledge this). Hence, claims that the Herfindahl index does not reflect cost considerations is misleading. Similarly, given everything else constant, a higher elasticity of demand implies a higher market share. This can be demonstrated as follows. Return to a monopoly market. Let p(y) be the price per unit and C(y) the cost of production. Then, profit maximization occurs at output y such that

$$p(y)\,[1 - (1/\eta)] = MC(y)$$

Differentiate both sides w.r.to η. This results in

$$[dp/dy\ \{1 - (1/\eta)\} - dMC/dy]\ dy/d\eta = -\ p(y)/\eta^2$$

It is well known that

$$\eta > 1,\ dp/dy < 0, \text{ and } dMC/dy > 0$$

It follows that $dy/d\eta > 0$.

(In section 3.6 below a new measure of market power will be defined integrating the Lerner measure with market shares. It will then be possible to show that such a measure of market power would move in tandem with the elasticity of demand).

3.3. Welfare Theoretic Interpretation

Dansby and Willig (1979) offered a welfare theoretic interpretation of the Herfindahl index. They construct a measure of sensitivity of social welfare to the locally best choices in output of a firm to arrive at such a result. Let $y(t)$ represent a vector of outputs y_i; $i = 1, 2, ..., n$ at any time t. Let y_0 be its initial configuration. Similarly, let $W\{y(t)\}$ be the welfare associated with the choice of $y(t)$. Then, maximizing the limit of

$[W\{y(t)\} - W(y)]/t$ as $t \rightarrow 0$ along the welfare gradient yields
φ = industry performance gradient
$= [\,\sum \{p - MC\ (y_i)\}^2/p^2]^{1/2}$

Assuming that the industry is a homogeneous oligopoly it represents the distance between the components $L_i = \{p - MC\ (y_i)\}/p$. That is, it is related to the Lerner measure of market power for each of the firms. Φ can also be interpreted as the welfare increment per unit distance.

Given the Cournot homogeneous oligopoly assumption it follows that $L_i = s_i/\eta$, where, as before

s_i = market share of i, and η = elasticity of demand.

Consequently, it follows that

$$\varphi^2 = H/\eta^2$$

On the other hand, the Lerner measure

$L = \sum s_i^2 / \eta$

This is basically the relationship between the two measures of market power.

Clearly, H will indicate the sensitivity of welfare to locally optimal output adjustments of firms. It should, however, be noted that it does not represent the global welfare performance of the industry. Though Dansby and Willig (1979) constructed the index taking possible conjectural variations among firms into account it is not relevant for the present purpose.

It is pertinent to note that the aspersions of Syverson (2019) that H does not take costs into account and that it has no welfare theoretic basis, are totally misplaced. However, it should be recalled that the welfare basis of L, rather than market power, was the basis of the criticism in Elzinga and Mills (2011). It appears that even the Herfindahl index can be interpreted as a welfare measure in the industry. In such a case it is an indicator of welfare rather than market power. The entire literature appears to be a circular argument without any clear way of breaking out of the impasse.

3.4. The Linda Index

The other popular measure based on s_i is the Linda (1976) index. One of the advantages of this approach is that the cutoff for the number of firms that mark the boundary of high concentration is made endogenous. It proceeds along the following lines.

1. Assume that the industry in question consists of n firms. Let s_i ; $i = 1, 2, ..., n$ represent the market share of firm i. Arrange the index of the firms in descending order of s_i beginning with the highest and ending with the lowest.
2. Define $S_m = \sum s_i$; $m = 1,2, ...,n$
3. Choose any $m \geq 2$. Compute
$E_i = (m-i)\, S_i / i\, (S_m - S_i)$
$E_i^* = E_i / m$
$L_m = \sum E_i^* / (m-1)$ where the summation is from 2 through m
since $(m-1)$ values are picked up.
4. Repeat the calculation of L_m for $m = 1, 2, ..., n$
5. Identify the M for which L_m is the lowest.

The Linda logic considers that the first M firms in the industry are likely to have market dominance. According to Linda (1976) this happens when the "the next firm is much smaller."

Further, a competitive market is represented by $s_i = 1/n$, i.e., all firms are of equal size. All the corresponding Linda indices will be 1/n. This indicates that none of the n firms has any market dominance. Similarly, in the specific case where the L index, instead of continuing to decrease, suddenly rises, the size gap suggests the oligopolistic nature of the group of firms.

Define

$L_s = \sum L_m / (M - 1)$ where the summation is from 2 through M.

Linda (1976) notes that

> " the numerical analyses already carried out have shown that the index L_s = .20 shows the existence of a relatively large and unbalanced oligopolistic arena in which competition is working satisfactorily, while an index L_s greater than the value of .5 shows that there is excessive 'oligopolistic density' which could act as an obstacle to competition. An L_s more than 1.000 would point to the existence of a high degree of dominance." – (Linda, 1976, 23)

Consider the following examples to provide an idea about the operation of this index.

Example 1:

$s_1 = .4$, $s_2 = .3$, $s_3 = .15$, $s_4 = .1$, and $s_5 = .05$

The computed values of L_m are

$L_2 = .665$, $L_3 = .690$, $L_4 = .650$, and $L_5 = 3.18$

The first four firms have market dominance. For this case $L_s = .668$ indicating the existence of an oligopolistic tendency.

Example 2:

$s_1 = .5$, $s_2 = .3$, $s_3 = .15$, and $s_4 = .05$

The computed values of L_m are

$L_2 = .835$, $L_3 = .446$, and $L_4 = 1.120$

Consequently, it can be inferred that the first three firms have market dominance. In this context L_s = .427 thereby suggesting that there is no significant market power.

A causal observation about these two examples suggests that (M – 1) firms have market dominance. It may be necessary to modify Linda's inference. Further, the market power calculation has no operational interpretation as such. This index has not been utilized in practice though it has an advantage in isolating the number of firms that have market dominance.

In general, it is difficult to say that there is an economic basis for the construction and interpretation of the index.

3.5. Some Adjustment

Another problem, though both L and H indices share this, corresponds to the multi-product nature of most firms. The H index simply adds up the revenue of each product to construct the total revenue while conceptualizing the market share. It would perhaps be desirable if product level indices can be conceptualized. As Rao (2009) pointed out, such multi-dimensional Herfindahl indices can be defined.

The recognition that by the nature of product markets, in which differentiated but substitutable products are sold, the net market power of each firm and the industry as a whole consist of the contribution of the market as it reflects the interaction with the consumers and the addition to it due to insufficient competitive response, that do not completely neutralize the advantages of all the firms, must be reflected in the market power index chosen ultimately.

In general, due to operational convenience, at any rate, the Hefindahl index should be preferred though with the usual caveats in perspective.

3.6. A new Index

As noted earlier, the nature of the market is such that each firm derives its market power both in its relationship with consumers on the market as well as its distinct advantages in its interaction with other firms. This is unlike the usual assumption that competition among firms cannot bestow any market power to firms since the product is the same across firms. Hence, the Lerner measure should be combined with market shares to obtain an appropriate composite index. The following measure accomplishes this.

To begin with let the Lerner measure for each firm be calculated utilizing the modification suggested by Hall (1998). Refer to chapter 2 for details. That is, υ_i and $s_{\pi\, i}$ can be computed for each firm and the index of market power of firm i can be defined as

$$I_i = \upsilon_i\, s_i \,/\, (1 - s_{\pi\, i})$$

since the L index should be multiplied by the s_i representing the market share of firm i in the total revenue of all firms in the industry. This can be elucidated further in the following manner. Observe that, by definition, L_i captures only the interaction between the consumers and the market. In general, it indicates the markup over marginal cost per unit revenue of the firm. The market power of firm i would also depend on the share of its revenue in the total sales of the firm since in the ultimate analysis a market power index is sought. In other words, the market share of the firm represents the interaction of the firm with the rivals in the market. In effect, the amount of influence of firm i, revealed by the Lerner measure, on the overall market power is in proportion to its market share. This is the rationale behind using I_i as the index of market power of a firm. The welfare implications of the Lerner measure are also not altered.

The market power index can now be computed as

$$H = \sum I_i\, s_i = \sum \upsilon_i\, s_i^2 \,/\, (1 - s_{\pi\, i}) = \sum v_i\, s_i^2, \text{ where } v_i = \upsilon_i \,/\, (1\text{-}s_{\pi i})$$

Once again, the market power of a firm carries over to the industry level only to the extent of its market share. For, while defining the market level index the interaction of the firm with the rivals in the market must be accounted for. Obviously, this method accounts for the economic interpretation of the square term as well as the appropriate economic meaning for the weights assigned.

Note that this index is consistent with the expectations in some extreme cases. First, suppose $s_i = 1/n$ for all i. This is the legally accepted characterization of a competitive market. In such a case, there is no between firm market power. Hence, only the market power due to the interaction of each firm with the consumers matters to all of them. Note that $I_i = v_i /n$ for all i. This is the essential spirit of the Lerner measure. Similarly, $I = \sum v_i\, s_i = \sum v_i /n$. There is no variation of I_i between firms. Second, assume that $s_i =$ 1 for one i and = 0 for all other i. Clearly, firm i is a monopoly. Its market power is the same as that of the industry. This can be easily verified. For, note that $I_i = v$ for that i. (Recall that $v = \eta / (\eta - 1)$). Third, suppose the only difference between the firms is their market shares. It will be expected that $I_i = v\, s_i$, and $I = v \sum s_i^2$. This corresponds to the intuitive expectation. The fourth intuitive context is that of homogeneous oligopoly. In this context the elasticity of demand for all the products is assumed to be the same, say η. Then it follows that the new index will be proportional to H.

Clearly this index is amenable to easy measurement. Defined in this manner I_i can also be utilized as the firm level market power index.

The following result is significant as was pointed out in section 3.3. Consider the composite index of market power of firm i

$$I_i = v_i\, s_i$$

It can be verified that

$$dI_i / d\eta_i = (v_i s_i / \eta_i)\,(\varepsilon_s - \varepsilon_L)$$

where ε_s and ε_L are the elasticities of v_i and s_i w.r.to η_i. It can be concluded that I_i decreases with η_i if $\varepsilon_s > \varepsilon_L$. This result is consistent with the requirement stipulated by Syverson (2019).

3.7. Overview

It is by now clear that the market shares of firms signal the market power of a firm in relation to its rivals in the industry. As such, in addition to its relation to the customers on the market, it contributes to the overall market power of a firm. Even so, it is necessary to acknowledge that the market shares are a consequence of non-price choices. Hence, such advantages can be captured equivalently by measures like the average cost of a firm relative to the average of all other firms. Similarly, selling expenses of firm i/ average selling expenses of rivals may be significant. Such indices reflect the advantage of a firm relative to rivals in the market.

It is important to note another aspect. Firms use non-price strategies to signal the value of their product to the consumers. Hence, a part of the increase in the market share of a firm is attributable to this property. For purposes of regulatory action this quantity should be accounted for while calculating the market power index.

Two other observations are in order. First, the market shares of several non-price strategies may replace the share of revenues usually employed. Clearly, the choice depends on the use to which the index is developed. Second, only some strategies of firms may be relevant in defining the market power of a firm. The identification of dominance of strategies and their implications for market power will be outlined in chapter 5.

It must also be recorded that computing Herfindahl indices at the firm level do not provide any information on the sources of such market power. It is necessary to develop market power measures at the level of each of the non-price strategies and then aggregate them to obtain the firm level market power if the application warrants it. Similarly, it would be essential to develop regulatory measures at the level of individual non-price strategies as well as that of a firm.

CHAPTER 4

NON-PRICE STRATEGIES

"Price alone does not define whether a deal is good. Attention to detail can reveal that a cheap price is not a bargain and, alternatively, that sometimes a higher price can be a better value. Even more significant is that business has reliable ways of determining when a transaction is desirable" - (Smith and Thurman, 2007, 14).

Abstract

This chapter attempts to define the nature and classification of non-price decisions. Their effects on the extent of the fulfillment of different objectives of the firm have been detailed. Various aspects, in addition to price cost margins and market shares, that qualify as measures of market power of the firm have been elaborated.

4.1. The Nature

The classical specification in economic theory postulates small firms in a market offering a uniform product produced at the same cost and offered at an identical price. The limit on the size of the firm may be due to technologically defined economies of scale. The efficiency in devising organizational arrangements and the limitations in attracting the requisite finances may also limit the size of the firm.

It has long been recognized that small differences in products, brought about by various factors like quality, presentation, sales effort and so on, provide each of the firms a certain degree of market dominance over rival firms. This may be considered as the beginning of the acknowledgment regarding non-price decisions of firms. The variety is a non-price strategy when it is acknowledged that markets have many firms producing differentiated products. In addition, differences in the cost of producing goods, various methods of distribution and marketing strategies of firms qualify as non-price decisions. A few of these details will be outlined.

Differences in the size of firms and the concomitant variations in the cost of production had a prominent role in firms distinguishing their product from those of others. For instance, Chandler (1990, ch.2) documented the important role of economies of scale in providing a firm its market dominance. Ellickson (2006), in addition, noted that fixed assets of large firms and the corresponding lower average costs explain why some markets remain highly concentrated.

The sale of a combination of many products may offer cost advantages for any one firm's product due to sharing of fixed costs. In addition, the consumers may find it advantageous to buy substitutable and/or complementary products from the same firm rather than procure them from different firms. This provides dominance to a firm offering a variety of related products.

Apart from technology, the advantages may be from the scope offered by the flexibility of capital stock, commitment to organizational goals, sourcing of inputs and loyalty of suppliers, logistic costs of warehousing, inventories, and transportation costs and so on. In the early literature, Marshall (1920, 240-322) provided a detailed list of non-price strategies that affect the costs of a firm.

A few more non-price strategies that affect the supply side include the quality of the product, packaging and presentation and the loyalty of input suppliers. Porter (1980, 1985) additionally documented the details of the supply chain management of the firm as a factor that contributed to the market dominance of firms. In general, following the strategic management literature, it can be claimed that the resource base of the firm and its core competence determines the market dominance of the firm.

As Frei and Morris (2012) observed, there are many organizational aspects that can be called non-price decisions. It would be difficult to enumerate all (or most) of them and provide an operational expression to their implementation.

Capitalizing on consumer preferences may offer sustained and long run advantages to a firm. Porter's (1980, 1985) paradigm of competitive advantage emphasized this phenomenon. On the other hand, McGrath (2013) argued that there is a wide spectrum of shifting consumer tastes and transient requirements that firms can cater to profitably. Markets are thus considered as dynamic arenas where firms can grow by entering new industries or repositioning themselves in other segments within the industry.

Location advantages do provide firms market dominance from the demand side. In general, consumers have some search costs (to locate the most suitable products and the firm that provides it) as well as transportation and financing costs to reach the sales outlet of the firm with the finances necessary to buy the desired quantity of the product. Loyalty of customers, to the products of the firm, depend on these factors and experience of the customer in the features that the product delivers in relation to the promises of the firm. However, large firms do not always have an advantage.

In the final analysis, the range of non-price strategies is very vast. It depends on the industry under consideration. Hence, any general theory will be subject to severe limitations.

The current market environment, in which firms are operating, is determined by the radical developments in microelectronics, the internet and the digital revolution. In this milieu new and unconventional patterns of non-price strategies are emerging. Identifying the efficiency of such strategies and the market power that any one firm has is warranted so that useful guidelines about the changing requirements can be provided to the managers of firms as well as public policy. As of now the only recognition is that effective implementation of strategies matter as much as their choice.

4.2. Their Effects

The assumption that the volume of sales will be fixed as soon as the price is revealed may be valid only if it can be assumed that the non-price choices of the firm have no effect on the market for the products of the firm. When there are many non-cooperative rivals in the market their attempts to utilize non-price strategies to gain superiority must be accounted for. Similarly, given the variety of differentiated products offered on the market the consumers may have difficulty in evaluating the value of products and make purchase decisions accordingly. For all practical purposes, consumers have asymmetric information about the extent to which a specific variety of the product satisfies their requirement. They try to ascertain the value of the products through their search process. On the other hand, firms utilize non-price strategies to provide necessary information to the consumers. Either of them may, up to a limit, help the customer discover the real value of the commodity. To that extent, at any rate, such costs have a positive value to the consumers.

However, non-price strategies, even when firms can maintain some distinctiveness and superiority, can be easily traced out and imitated to reduce the market dominance of a firm. On the other hand, it would be more difficult to imitate product line choices. Similarly, strategies that can promote the goodwill of consumers, workers, input suppliers and marketing agents may be far more difficult to compete away since they are intangible and difficult to reduce once they have taken root.

In either case, as Gundlach and Moss (2018) suggested, the differences in quality, variety and provision of services, novelty of innovation, method of distribution, and increased product variety may be enhancing the value that customers derive from the product that they buy. However, an increase in market power may arise due to non-price choices of firms adversely affecting consumers. This may include product quality, reduced product variety, or reduced service. Further, when the fixed assets of a firm are large, they may lead to a high market share (not necessarily high profits) and thereby reduce the prospects of entry and stifle innovation of new products.

One further observation is in order. The multi-dimensional nature of non-price strategies needs attention both in isolation as well as in developing a procedure for aggregation. As a practical matter just defining the best service at the macro level and trying to deliver it will not be of much use. Instead, firms should start at the micro level, choose the best and implement as many variations as possible.

4.3. Value Generation

One of the prominent advantages of non-price competition alluded to above was the identification by the consumer of the value of a product sought to be bought. It is necessary to identify the amount of the non-price choice which assists this search versus the extent to which it creates market power.

This can be attempted in the following manner. Let x denote the quantity of the non-price measure. It helps the consumer in identifying the value of the product. Let $V(x) = Vx$ be the value. The expectation is that the true value will be revealed when $x = x^*$. The consumer will not pay a higher price. It is also not possible to conceptualize increasing the value of the product beyond this. Assume that $V(x^*) = Vx^*$ persists even if the firm increases its spending on the non-price strategy until $x = m$ where m is a conceptual maximum.

Clearly, the firm incurs a cost in implementing its choice. Let $C(x)$ be the cost. It may be postulated as $C(x) = Cx$. It would be realistic to assume that $V > C$. For, otherwise, it would not be economical for the firm to adopt the strategy. Let x_1 denote the value of x such that $V(x) = C(x)$. It can be verified that $x_1 = Vx^*/C > x^*$. Only when $x > x_1$ can it be said that the choice of non-price strategy is excessive in the sense that C(x) exceeds the value of the product to the consumer.

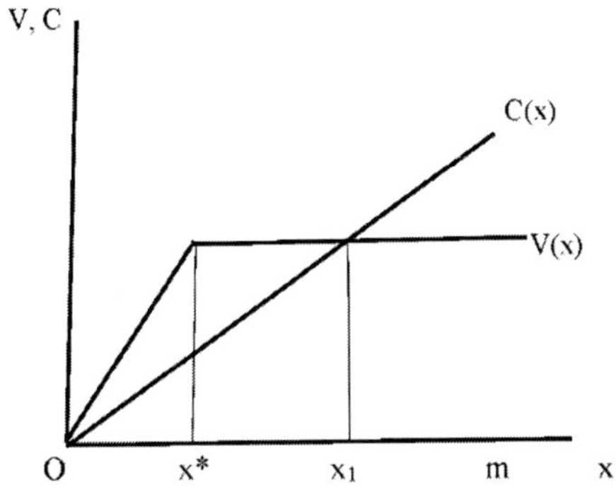

Fig. 1

It is important to consider the reasons for the firms and/or the consumers accepting an increase in x from x* until x_1 or beyond. If $V_x > C_x$ for any given $x < x_1$ the firm may just as well reduce the quality of the product instead of increasing signaling. However, given the competitive nature of rival choices firms would prefer to be defensive. Further, though there is a reduction in the price cost margins the improvement in the market share may give them larger overall profits. The increase in the market power attributable to larger market shares may add to the firms accepting it. Similarly, the consumers would be willing to accept the firm expanding its non-price choices to x_1. For, there is an increase in value, over the cost of the non-price choice, until $x = x_1$. By the same token any regulatory activity that tries to reduce x to x* will imply a loss of welfare to the consumer. Indeed, the consumer may accept this reduction in the price cost margins of the firm and the corresponding increase in market share. In general, it should be expected that x will increase until x_1.

Some properties of x* may now be recorded. Let m denote the maximum amount of non-price strategy that the firm can use given its capabilities and resources. The total value generated is given by $Vx^*m - Vx^{*2}/2$. Let the firm expect a total revenue T from the sale of the product depending on the resources and capabilities of the firm. The following results are automatic.

An increase in V makes x* larger. For, greater efforts should be put in to identify the true value of the product. This can be readily verified by noting that, ceteris paribus,

$$dx^*/dV = x^* (2m - x^*)/ 2Vx^* > 0.$$

Secondly, let m increase. The consumer may visualize the possibility that the product is of lower quality since the firm is putting in a larger amount of effort to sell the product. This implies that x* will fall. Notice that

$$dx^*/dm = x^*/ (x^* - m) < 0$$

corroborates this. Let T increase instead. The possibility is that the capacity to generate greater total value will induce the firm to expect x* to rise. For, note that $dx^*/dT = 1/ V (m - x^*) > 0$. It should be noted that throughout this analysis it was assumed that the firm would signal value initially and the consumer will accept or reject it. The final value will be revealed only when the consumer accepts the offer by the firm.

The estimation of x* is a crucial issue while appraising the role of non-price strategies. An alternative to estimating market power would be available if it can be estimated. The following method suggests itself. Define the probability density function over (0,m) as $f(x) = x$ if $x < x^*$, and $= x^*$ for $x^* \leq x \leq m$, where m is the maximum value of the non-price characteristic that the firm chooses. In order that this is a pdf over the support (0, m) it is necessary to choose $m = (1+x^{*2})/2x^*$. Conversely, x* can be made a function of m. However, the issue of choosing m will be unresolved. Essentially, the parameters, viz., m and x* should be estimated simultaneously. The necessary additional information can be obtained from the sample average of x_i; i = 1,2..., n. Denote it by x_m.. Using this information x* can be solved from the equation $x^{*4} - 12 x^{*2} + 24 x_m x^* - 12 = 0$. In any practical application it should be expected that x* will depend on v. Hence, f(x) can be redefined as $f(x) = vx$ for $x < x^*$ and $= vx^*$ for $x^* \leq x \leq m$ and the above procedure repeated. Note that v can also be estimated by utilizing the second moment from the sample. vx_l and vx^* associated with it will provide the necessary information to define the market power of the non-price choice of the firm.

Several other methods have been proposed. A sample of such studies is Goldfeld and Quandt (1973), Petrucilli (1986), Porter (2003), Klusowski et al (2019) and Hajivassiliou (2019). Obviously, C can be estimated as y_m /x_m where the y_m and x_m represent the sample averages.

This analysis does not compare the activities of the firm with its rivals. As such it cannot indicate the existence or otherwise of market power of the firm. That exercise should be taken up before any suggestions of regulatory action.

4.4. Objectives of the Firm

Profit maximization has practically become a benchmark for most of economic theorizing. However, several examples of the failure of single minded and unique goal pursuit have been documented. Glaring examples are of Kodak that concentrated on maximizing market share in the processing of film through a wide network of franchisees. It did not anticipate that the digital camera would undermine its existence. Similar examples are IBM with respect to PCs, newspapers and publishing generally, and even Microsoft that concentrated on its office suit for long and so on. Beattie (2009) documented many such instances. It is therefore essential that firms redefine their objectives while they strive to adjust their strategies to suit the shifting objectives made mandatory by the changing market environment.

Clearly, maximum profit may not be the objective of all firms. Typical examples include Baumol (1958,1959, 1982), Cyert and March (1963) and Marris (1964). Some firms may maximize market share, others may find large scale of capital and fixed assets necessary to achieve market dominance, and yet others may maximize the goodwill of consumers with a long run view of survival. Lutz (2013) argued that

> "At the end of the day, delivering results should be a leader's goal. And in business, it's shareholder's value, brought about by profitability, market share growth, corporate reputation and long term outlook." – (Lutz, 2013, 201)

Firms generally have a significant time horizon rather than merely think of a hit and run advantage. They may indeed be pursuing a variety of objectives simultaneously though with different degrees of emphasis. The best combination is continuously amended based on persistent bargaining and learning within the management and after a thorough examination of the user needs for their products. However, it should be clear, given the nature of competition, that each of the firms would be able to accomplish only a subset of the desired goals. For all practical purposes, the market power of any one firm may be due to the pursuit of one or more possible objectives.

Hence, firms should acknowledge that at any point of time two or more objectives may be substitutable (as they were perceived originally) or complementary (dictated by the shifting market landscape). Stated differently, firms should attempt a balance between the objectives they wish to pursue and those that changing consumer preferences signify. In the final analysis, as Tofflcr (1980) and Bolton et al (2014) pointed out, it is necessary to hold a larger perspective even while implementing small things so that they can be executed as required.

4.5. Mixed Markets

It was noted that some firms may choose two or more strategies in their attempt to establish market dominance. Such choices will have their corresponding market power. Instead of each of them having separate market power their combined effect may be more significant. A procedure to identify such joint impacts is necessary.

Suppose strategies i and j are complementary. Then, define a single strategy with a market share $s_i + s_j + s_i s_j$ and utilize it in measuring market power. Similarly, suppose a strategy i exists currently and another substitutable strategy j is sought to be introduced. Then, the market share of i may be reduced to $s_i/ (1+s_j)$ and the market share of j increased to $s_j / (1-s_i)$. Similarly, analogous to the above case, they can be combined to a single strategy with a market share $s_i + s_j - s_i s_j$ indicating that they cannibalize each other.

Once the existence of many characteristics around which firms differentiate their products is acknowledged, one of the important differences is in the conceptualization of what constitutes a monopoly firm or a competitive set of firms. The following generalization attempts to improve the above procedures.

Consider the issue of comparing the monopoly power exercised by two firms, one of which is a monopoly and the other one from a competitive group of n firms. Let $s_i = 1$and = 0 with respect to firms in the other cluster. Similarly, $s_j = 1/n$ with respect to the competitive cluster and = 0 with respect to the other represent their market shares. Consequently, it can be inferred that

m_i = market power of i relative to the competitive group
$= s_i^2 - s_j^2 = 1$

Similarly,

$$m_j = s_j^2 - s_i^2 = 1/n^2$$

That is, the ith firm retains its monopoly power with respect to such a competitive firm.

Consider two firms from distinct competitive clusters. Let $s_i = 1/n$ and = 0 in the other cluster. Similarly, let $s_j = 1/m$ and = 0 in the other where the number of firms in each of the clusters is n and m respectively. Hence, once again, the market power of firm i is

$m_i = 1/n^2$ and similarly
$m_j = 1/m^2$ under similar conditions.

Hence, both retain their market power. They can be classified as monopolies with respect to the other group.

It can be readily verified that these results hold generally when comparing (a) a monopoly firm with one firm from a competitive cluster, (b) two firms from distinct competitive clusters, (c) two firms that are monopolies, or (d) a monopoly against another firm that is not from the group of monopoly firms or any of the competitive clusters.

Many other cases have been detailed in Rao (2009). However, it would not be worthwhile to reproduce those results here.

Throughout the study the emphasis was on price cost margins and/or market shares as the central concern of the firms. This was taken as a foregone conclusion. However, in some markets large capital assets may be required to achieve possible economies of scale and scope. In such contexts it may not be possible to improve profits or market shares given the market constraints on the extent of demand for the products. In general, firms may agree to forego profits and/or market shares in the short run to obtain dynamic advantages. Indeed, the firm may have dynamic advantages when the markets are growing and/or have the advantages of barriers to entry. The market power so derived is both qualitatively and quantitatively different. Similarly, the nature of products and the technologies embodied therein are changing significantly. Firms would prefer to make the necessary dynamic adjustments even if they must forego some profits or accept reduced market shares in the short run. In the dynamic context firms would also prefer to develop loyalties of customers, input suppliers, workers, and marketing agents in preference to short run considerations of high profits and/or market shares. In many contexts the adjustments in organizational arrangements and distribution strategies to improve market shares may involve rather significant changes in costs. In such cases a balance will have to be chosen. In general, when considering markets where firms sell differentiated products it becomes necessary to be vigilant to the possibility of unexpected objectives pursued by firms. The current theories and measurement of market power are unequal to such tasks.

The most important observation is that in the type of market under consideration each of the firms will have a distinct profile that need not fit into a pattern across other firms in the industry. The analysis of their strategies, market power and associated regulatory policies should proceed at the firm level rather than consider aggregates at the industry level. Clearly, such an analysis will exclude some firms from regulatory action.

When viewed from a broader perspective non-price strategies may be classified as belonging to those that provide production and cost advantages to a firm vs. those that provide value information to consumers and alter the demand for the products of a firm. The firm may also consider loyalties of various types as significant from a long run perspective. It would be necessary to limit them further by identifying market dominance of specific choices. Great many details of non-price strategies may not be particularly useful.

Even after some non-price choices are identified as important from the viewpoint of a firm it would be necessary to single out the value maximizing extent of the choices. The market power of a firm over and above that implied by such choices would be of concern to the consumers and regulators. It is this context that directs analysis to identify them explicitly. The consumers may themselves find certain non-price choices as more significant indicators of the value of the products to them. It is difficult to find a mechanism through which they can convey this information to the firms let alone make the firms accept such choices.

There are many candidates for the objectives of a firm. Clearly, any one firm may pursue one of them or a combination of several of them according to some lexicographic ordering. It would be useful to identify the priorities of each of the firms that will determine their market power relative to rivals. As with non-price strategies, only pursuit of select objectives may be providing the market power that a firm has. It would be useful to separate them.

It is also evident that the relationship between the objectives of the firm, their non-price strategies, and the basic determinants of the nature of the market require further study. Market power indices that will be detailed in chapter 6 would provide adequate guidelines.

CHAPTER 5

MARKET DOMINANCE

"Google can only see patterns programmed into its algorithms, while our minds can synthesize the nuances of a question to connect dots, that, at times, weren't at all expected. Having a larger data set in our minds and experience may allow us to come up with more discerning answers." - (Conley, 2018, 137).

Abstract

To begin with a distinction has been made between the strategies that the firm wishes to choose to attain market dominance and what it can achieve given the reactions of non-cooperative rival firms. Three distinct methods of identifying dominant strategies of firms have been detailed. The primary distinction between the methods is their ability to isolate one or more choices of a firm that provide it the market dominance that it has. An example illustrates the differences between the methods. It is important to note that the shift in analysis is from the industry level to clearly identifiable strategies at the firm level.

5.1. The Idea of Dominance

The foregoing chapters presented a case to recognize the significance of the non-price strategies of firms and their consequences both for the firms and consumer welfare. This chapter will be devoted exclusively to the notion of market dominance and its identification.

Economic theory does not generally make any distinction between market power and market dominance. Even in markets characterized as differentiated oligopoly it is taken for granted that differences in the elasticity of demand for different products is the only source that provides market dominance and the associated market power. Non-price strategies of firms are not supposed to have any separate and independent effect.

However, a firm can be deemed to have market dominance if its strategies suggest that they are quantitatively or qualitatively superior from those of rivals. Identifying the dominant choices will be important to correlate them with the sources of market power that a firm has. In general, the market dominance of a firm may be in the form of its choices that provide it demand and/or cost advantages vis-a-vis its rivals.

Kinght (1965) argued that firms develop dominance due to their ability to adapt faster to unexpected events. For, it was suggested that

> "sincc production should be ahead of demand a firm may have a monopoly in anticipating future market requirements and making plans to fulfill them. For, men differ in their capacity to perception and inferences to form correct judgments as to the future course of events in the environment." (Knight, 1965,241)

While this is conceptually elegant it does not provide an operationally useful method of delimiting the dominant strategies of each firm in the market.

Porter (1980, 1985) indicated that the market dominance of any firm depends not only on the choices of product lines but also on how they are implemented. For, having made a product line choice the management must organize production and the inbound and outbound logistics efficiently. Though these studies provided a great many details that need attention they did not indicate any specific methods of choice for different firms that encounter differing situations.

Crilly (2014) suggested that every firm operating in differentiated oligopoly endeavors to devise and implement strategies consistent with its objectives depending on the dynamic position already achieved and its perception of opportunities and threats from rivals. However, quite independent of the causation between strategies and market power, it is necessary to identify the choices that constitute the sources of market dominance to begin with since they will be the target of public policy and/or changes in managerial strategies.

Recognizing such a need Classens (2009) pointed out the necessity to develop new concepts designed to address changes that are typical of the structure of differentiated oligopoly. A clear breakthrough from established practices is warranted to provide an approach to the notion, source, and extent of market dominance attributable to distinct strategic decisions of firms.

Bordean et al (2011) observed that a firm may dominate with respect to a few strategies and utilize others to differentiate itself from others. The firm may also adopt selected strategies primarily to avoid being surpassed by rivals. See, for example, Yannopoulus (2011) and Larsen (2014). Two observations are pertinent. First, Fischer and Kamerschen (2003 a,b) argued that the dominance of a firm cannot be explained by assuming that all of them compete along the same dimensions. Second, as Parnell (2006) contends, a strategy is conceptualized, very often, on anecdotal evidence that firms identified as unique to any one or a small group of firms within an industry. As of now there is no systematic analytical approach to make comparisons across firms to arrive at the optimal combination of strategies.

5.2. The Methods

While developing a suitable method it is important to recognize the distinction between what a firm wises to achieve and what it can accomplish given the reactions of rivals to its decisions. For, the realization of desires, rather than wishes themselves, will determine the results achieved by the firm. The following methods have been designed with this observation in perspective.

Method 1:

Let x_{ij} represent the value of the characteristic i for firm j, where i = 1, 2, ..., N and j = 1, 2, ..., n. Clearly, x_{ij} are comparable over j for a given i. Suppose a firm j wishes to achieve dominance with respect to its choice of i. It can be expected that it will choose the largest x_{ij} relative to others. When such a desire to superiority is established for every characteristic i it is possible to consolidate the strategies that firm j wishes to adopt. However, firm j can achieve superiority with respect to a strategy only if rivals allow it to do so. Suppose there is another firm k which is the nearest rival in the sense that x_{ik} is the next largest in comparison to x_{ij}. Define $r_{jk} = x_{ij}/x_{ik}$. Let firm j wish to achieve superiority w.r.to strategies α, β, γ etc. Suppose k, l, m etc are the corresponding near rivals. Choose the largest among $r_{\alpha k}$, $r_{\beta l}$ and $r_{\gamma m}$ etc. Firm j can achieve a dominant position w.r.to the corresponding strategy.

Clearly, the firm can be said to differentiate itself from a rival by choosing all other strategies through which it desires to achieve a position of superiority. Thus, every strategy that the firm chooses in its desire to obtain superiority will be either a dominant strategy or enable it to differentiate itself from them. This approach to identification was proposed in Rao (2017).

This method is particularly suitable if every firm pursues a unique strategy to achieve dominance. Other choices, even when they are made, are only to meant to differentiate itself from others and protect itself from being overtaken by rival firms. However, Yamin et al (1999) pointed out that a firm using a combination of two or more strategies to achieve market dominance tends to outperform those that adopt a single strategy. The following method considers the possibility that some firms utilize a single strategy while others may purse multiple strategies.

Method 2:

The first natural question is: which of the characteristics i does the firm wish to choose to achieve market dominance? Observe that s_{ij} defined above are all fractions that are independent of the dimensions of measurement. This makes them comparable over i for a given j. Compute, for any given j, $t_{ij} = s_{ij}/s_{.j}$ where $s_{.j} = \sum s_{ij}$ (i.e., the summation is over i). Suppose firm j wishes to achieve market dominance by choosing characteristic i. Clearly, it will be i = a for which t_{ij} is the maximum for the given j. Can firm α achieve dominance w.r.to i = a? It should be evident that this can be achieved if $s_{a\alpha}$ is the maximum over s_{ij}. In practice, this may not always hold. One meaningful inference in such a context is that firms use the characteristic for purely differentiating purposes. They leave the performance they achieve entirely to market forces hoping that they will survive for now to plan for achieving better performance in the future. It can also be inferred that firm α is not choosing the $x_{a\alpha}$ appropriately. This indicates a necessity for intervention by the management.

To make the above procedure operational, mark a s in each row for which s_{ij} is the maximum. Similarly, insert a t in each column for which t_{ij} is the maximum. Consider any firm α. If both t and s appear for a given combination (a, α) it can be inferred that firm α wishes to choose strategy a and it is able to achieve dominance given the non-cooperative environment. On the other hand, if for any α, t appears in the column for strategy a and there is a s corresponding to strategy b it can be inferred that firm α uses strategy b to differentiate itself from other firms. Clearly, every firm utilizes other strategies purely for defensive purposes (maintain their visibility) to stay clear of encroachment by rivals.

The major patterns that are likely and their interpretation may now be considered. Construct the Nxn matrices S and T alluded to above. Conceptually though a s may occur in any one column in every row it will appear in at least one column. A similar observation applies for the occurrence of t as well. Generally, several non-price strategies are discernible. As a result, s may occur in many rows corresponding to a given α. This indicates the possibility that a firm may utilize two or more non-price strategies in its quest for dominance. Consider the unlikely possibility that a s appears in every column corresponding to strategy a. Strictly speaking it cannot be interpreted to mean that every firm can achieve dominance with respect to a. Instead, it should be construed as an indication that none of the firms has any strategic advantage. Hence, there is every reason to believe that different firms tend to pursue different strategies. To think that majority of firms can succeed in pursuing the same strategies may not be particularly attractive. Usually diversity is the key that provides the firms the strategic dominance they have.

More to the point, the number of combinations (Nxn) is bewilderingly large. A few representative configurations will be highlighted in what follows. Every other possible outcome will have to be interpreted with great caution.

The above enumeration of patterns of market dominance can as well be w.r.to the product line choice or non-price strategies.

Clearly this procedure provides a distinction between the following possibilities. (a) The firm achieves what it wishes to accomplish w.r.to one or more of the choices for which it seeks dominance. (b) The firm can only achieve a subset of the choices. It should be possible to specify the course correction to the managerial choices that can bring about a movement in the right direction. (c) None of the strategies that the firm targets may be implementable in the face of non-cooperative reactions of rivals. The management is inefficient.

The alternative that every firm chooses a combination of two or more strategies in its attempt to achieve dominance may be explored by adopting a different method.

Method 3:

Suppose every firm utilizes two or more strategies to achieve dominance. For all practical purposes, a firm can be conceptualized as using all strategies that do not differ from each other by more than 1/N since there are N characteristics to choose from. Similarly, all firms, whose s_{ij} values do not differ by more than 1/n can be deemed to be using those strategies to achieve dominance. As before, the (t, s) characterization will identify all the strategies that a firm wishes to and achieve against competitive rivals.

The classical description is that as n increases the firms become more competitive. Instead, this analysis indicates that smaller n enables each firm to assess the activities of others and remain competitive. On the other hand, when n is large the firms will find it difficult to ascertain the choices of others and develop a countervailing response. Under these conditions some firms may gain greater market dominance. The new environment of non-competitive firms does not sustain the usual competitiveness paradigm.

In the ultimate analysis the method which the management will choose to pursue must be left to their discretion.

5.3. An Illustrative Example

Such methods isolate all the characteristics w.r.to which firm j can achieve dominance as well as those that it utilizes to differentiate itself from the rivals. However, notice that the methods presented here are very general and apply to all industries. Industries and firms differ in significant ways. Hence, the feeling is that presenting empirical work related to any one or more industries will shift the emphasis to their idiosyncrasies and undermine the strength of the generality of the economic theory developed here. Hence, this section will present a hypothesized example (the definition of the variables and the data are presented in the appendix) to appreciate the workings of the methods in practice.

The results for the illustrative example are detailed below. Note that non-price strategies have been classified into those based on product characteristics and all others. This is motivated by the observation that product characteristics will generally have deeper implications for the improvement in consumer welfare. To be sure, there will be some choices that enhance the market power of firms more prominently.

Non-Price Strategies (Product Characteristics)

Method 1:

The variables that provide dominance for each firm are listed below. For the example presented here, firms appear to seek and maintain dominance with respect to Organization of Production (F1), Product Variety (F2), Franchising (F3), Subsidiaries (F4), Fashion Goods (F5), and Easy to Integrate Products (F6). In addition, F1 utilizes Complementary and Substitutable Products and F3 utilizes attainment of Economies of scale and Scope as differentiating strategies.

Method 2:

	F1	F2	F3	F4	F5	F6
VR		(t,s)				
CSP	s					
FG					(t,s)	
ESS			s			
MPP	(t,s)					
EI						(t,s)
FR			(t,s)			
SU				(t,s)		

Firms seek dominance w.r.to offering a sufficiently large product variety, choose products that can be easily integrated into their existing production lines, and in some cases fashion goods. Organizing production through franchising or subsidiaries have been the preferred strategies. While the choices exhibited by method 1 remain invariant this method suggests that F1 can have an advantage w.r.to complementary products, and F3 has an advantage w.r.to products offering economies of scale and scope. The management will do well to recognize this in their decision process. This method signals that it may be best for each firm to choose the top two strategies and ensure that they can be sustained.

Method 3:

	F1	F2	F3	F4	F5	F6
VR		(t,s)		(t,s)		
CSP	(t,s)			s		
FG					(t,s)	(t,s)
ESS			(t,s)		s	
MPP	(t,s)	(t,s)				
EI					(t,s)	(t,s)
FR			(t,s)	s		
SU				(t,s)		

As expected, the firms do indeed intend to use strategies that were characterized as s by method 2. The important observation based on this method is that all firms have dominance w.r.to two or more strategies. As noted earlier, the managements do consider the strategies marked as s earlier are important. This method makes them belong to the (t,s) category.

None of the firms in this example were such that a t alone appears for any one firm corresponding to a strategy. This would imply that though the management wishes to achieve dominance w.r.to that strategy they are not paying attention to its implementation. This managerial inefficiency may eventually result in the closure of the firm if corrective action is not initiated.

Non-Price Strategies

Method 1:

F1 has dominance w.r.to LOC, F2 has dominance w.r.to ISR while F3's advantage is w.r.to DP. Similarly, F4 gains by using OS, F5 has an advantage w.r.to PD and F6 has its advantage in choosing BP. Further, the differentiating strategies are: MO and DE (F1), AD (F2), DU (F4), and RS (F6). Having sufficient supplies in market locations, to maintain adequate inventories and paying suppliers only after their products are sold (akin to Walmart's business policy) and online sales exhibit dominance in this example. Advertisements and making sure that selling outlets get their supplies on time are the differentiating strategies. Of equal importance are the financial arrangements to conduct their business.

The following table presents the strategic dominance revealed by method 2.

Method 2:

	F1	F2	F3	F4	F5	F6
BP						s
ISR		s				
MO	s					
PD					(t,s)	
DU				s		
ADV		(t,s)				
DP			(t,s)			
OS				(t,s)		
LOC	s					
RS						(t,s)
DE	(t,s)					(t,s)

Many differentiating strategies have been adopted by these firms, though they do not seem to explicitly attempt dominance. Strategies like advertising, durability and warranties for their products are in this category.

Similarly, the dominant strategies suggested by method 3 are exhibited in the table that follows.

Method 3:

	F1	F2	F3	F4	F5	F6
BP						(t,s)
ISR		(t,s)				
MO	(t,s)					
PD					(t,s)	
DU				(t,s)		s
ADV		(t,s)			(t,s)	
DP			(t,s)			
OS				(t,s)		
LOC	s					
RS						(t,s)
DE	(t,s)					

Method 3 acknowledges that firms may indeed recognize the need to pursue the dominant strategies marked as s in method 2. They attempt to seek dominance w.r.to these strategies.

Rao (2017) pointed out many other possible patterns in a different context. It is necessary to acknowledge that unique features may be present in every case under consideration.

In sum, this chapter presented a case to isolate strategies that provide market dominance to firms and suggested methods of isolating them. The role of such choices in determining market power will be considered in the next chapter.

Appendix

The Data

Objectives
1. Profit (PR)
2. Market Share (MS)
3. Price-Cost Margins (PCM)
4. Share Prices (SP)
5. Market Value (MV)

Non-Price Strategies (Product Characteristics)

Product Types
1.Variety (VR)
2.Complementary or Substitutable Products (CSP)
3. Fashion Goods (FG)

Technology and Organization
4. Economies of Scale and Scope (ESS)
5.Managerial Personnel/Production Workers (MPP)
6. Easy to Integrate in Production Line (EI)
7. Franchising (FR)
8. Subsidiaries (SU)

Non-Price Strategies (others)

Supply Side
1.Business Policy Toward Suppliers (BP)
2.Inventory/Sales Ratio (ISR)
3.Making Products Available to Marketing Outlets (MO)
4.Packaging and Display (PD)
5.Durability (DU

Demand Side
6.Advertising and Selling Costs (ADV)
7.Discounts and Promotions (DP)
8.Online Sales (OS)
9.Offering a Large Variety of Products (LOC)

Financial Arrangements
10.Reserves and Surpluses (RS)
11.Debt-Equity Ratio (DE)

The figures in the following tables are s_{ij} where the index i is used for the characteristics and j is for the firms denoted by F1 etc. Obviously, the row sums must be equal to 1 while the column sums need not be.

Objectives

	F1	F2	F3	F4	F5	F6
PR	.10	.51	.15	.12	.08	.04
MS	.45	.20	.12	.11	0.	.08
PCM	.19	.21	.40	.02	.10	.08
SP	.18	.15	.04	.42	.18	.03
MV	.10	.03	.20	.05	.47	.15

Product Characteristics

	F1	F2	F3	F4	F5	F6
VR	.15	.31	.12	.27	.07	.08
CSP	.33	.2	.11	.20	.14	.10
FG	.10	.05	.10	.05	.47	.23
ESS	.05	.15	.27	.20	.20	.13
MPP	.42	.20	.06	.10	.07	.15
EI	.10	.10	.12	.00	.27	.41
FR	.12	.10	.43	.20	.05	.10
SU	.1	.0	.10	.41	.10	.20

Non-Price Strategies

	F1	F2	F3	F4	F5	F6
BP	.13	.10	.15	.15	.10	.37
ISR	.11	.37	.10	.12	.15	.15
MO	.40	.10	.10	.10	.20	.10
PD	.12	.15	.13	.15	.35	.10
DU	.10	.10	.10	.37	.10	.23
ADV	.05	.40	.15	.10	.25	.05
DP	.15	.10	.41	.11	.08	.15
OS	.10	.15	.10	.40	.13	.12
LOC	.37	.10	.15	.15	.10	.13
RS	.05	.16	.22	.05	.10	.42
DE	.42	.10	.05	.22	.16	.05

CHAPTER 6

MARKET POWER

> "No matter how great and innovative your ideas are, and how hard you work, some will succeed and others won't. You cannot control exogenous events.... nor should you take credit for them when they benefit you." - (Lubetzky, 2015, p.112).

Abstract

Market power measurement, at the firm level and of their strategies, constitutes the core of this chapter. It was noted in an earlier chapter that non-price strategies can provide value addition to consumers. Hence, it was shown that certain low values of market shares would indeed satisfy this property. Utilizing this information along with firm level measures of market power indicate that a few firms have positive market power. The example of the previous chapter has been pursued to illustrate the implications of the proposed methods.

6.1. Market Power Issues

Efforts on the part of firms to maximize profits have been central to the characterization of market power. At the industry level, profits will be high either because it has higher price-cost margins and/or because of high market shares of some firms. One group of studies emphasizes high price-cost margins and/or changes in them consequent to certain choices by firms while the other centers around market shares at the firm level.

It should be noted that in much of the literature measures of market power have been developed mostly at the industry level. Further, market power was meant to be the advantage that firms have exclusively due to the imperfections in the product market. This is considered as the only appropriate definition. There is, however, increasing acknowledgment regarding the central role of non-price strategies in defining the differences in the elasticity of demand across firms. Price-cost margins have been defined at the firm level, albeit under the restrictive assumption of homogeneous oligopoly. Such measures can be aggregated to the industry level using market shares as the appropriate weights. However, studies based on market shares find even the conceptualization of the Herfindahl indices problematic in their attempts to define market power at the firm level.

Further, the underlying assumption of profit maximization has been questioned often. For, some firms may maximize market share and yet others maximize the market value of the firm and so on. Therefore, in general, market power may be in the form of a price in excess of the marginal cost of production, one that creates a greater than minimum cost of production, a level of advertising in excess of that required to provide the consumer information about the value of the product, utilize information about the 'likes' to target advertising which the consumer does not like and so on. It is not clear if either of the market power definitions is appropriate in all these contexts.

Neither of the conventional measures attempted to disentangle the sources of market power in detail. Further, it was recognized that aggregate measures, even those developed at the firm level, do not convey any information about the non-price choices that contribute to them. Differences in the elasticity of demand will be one aspect. The rival reactions in the market with differentiated products has an equally important role. An attempt would therefore be made to measure the market power of individual firms in the market taking both these aspects into account.

6.2. The Precedents

Defining indices to identify the market power at the firm level are rather scanty. However, a few attempts made earlier to define the market power of firms, as distinct from the industry level market power, do provide a broad guideline. It would therefore be useful to outline them to begin with.

Kiyota et al (2009) defined

m_j = market power of firm j
$= s_j^2 / \sum s_k^2$, where the summation is over $k \neq j$

It is not altogether clear if the choices of rival firms will have a multiplicative effect on m_j. If that is indeed valid the summation over $k \neq j$ cannot be justified. It is perhaps far more important to recognize that this measure cannot reveal any information about the managerial decision processes which account for it.

Rao (2012, 2015) proposed several other measures based on s_j. First,

$m_j = 1 - C_j / p_j s_j S$, where
C_j = cost of production of firm j, and $S = \sum y_i$.

Note that if $s_j = 1$ and $s_k = 0$ for all $j \neq k$ this measure reduces to

$m_j = (p_j - c_j)/p_j$, where c_j = average cost of firm j.

Second, since s_k^2/s_j^2 represents the competitiveness of firm k w.r.to j the market power of firm k relative to rivals can be written as

$$m_k = 1 - \sum s_j^2 / [s_k^2/(n-1)]$$

These measures cannot reveal the market power of individual non-price strategies.

Such a measurement can be approached analogously. Define

x_{ij} = value of characteristic i for firm j; i = 1, 2, ..., N and j = 1,2 ..., n, and
$s_{ij} = x_{ij} / \sum x_{ik}$, where the summation is over all k.

Rao (2015) proposed the measure

$$m_{ij} = 1 - \sum s_{il}^2 / (n-1)\, s_{ij}^2$$

where the summation is over $l \neq j$, and the expression $\sum s_{il}^2 / (n-1)$ is the average market power of each of the rival firms. Consider the obvious case where $s_{ij} = 1$ for j and $s_{il} = 0$ for all $l \neq j$. The value of $m_{ij} = 1$ indicating that firm j alone has the market power w.r.to characteristic i. On the other hand, if $s_{ij} = 1/n$ for all j, $m_{ij} = 0$ suggesting that none of the firms has any market power wr.to i. The difficulty with these measures is the same as with that of Kiyota et al (2009) since there is an ambiguity whether the effect of the reactions of rivals is additive or multiplicative.

An alternative measure proposed in Rao (2012) recognizes the relationship between firms and measures it using

$$\rho_{ij}^2 = s_{ij}(1 - s_{ij})/\sum s_{ij}^2$$

where the summation is over all j.

The effective market power of firm i w.r.to the characteristic j is then

$$m_{ij} = (1 - \rho_{ij}^2)\, s_{ij}^2$$

The above special cases of market power hold even relative to this definition. Similarly, the sources of market power of firm i remain elusive except in the extreme cases mentioned earlier.

It should also be noted that the measure suggested above is positive for all values of i. This may be a disadvantage when conceptualizing regulatory action. Instead, it would be useful to isolate a few firms as the major sources of market power in such a context. It would be necessary to identify them.

In retrospect, there is no specification of the non-price strategies that provide the firm the market power nor is there any operationally useful information about the market power that non-price strategies provide a firm. Further analysis is in order.

6.3. Some Pointers

The property developed in chapter 4, of firms enabling the consumers to discover the value of the products of the firm utilizing their non-price choices, will have to be taken into account while constructing the market power of the firm. However, it should be reiterated that such an analysis reflects the activities of a firm in isolation. Market power indices, that take the interaction of the firm with market forces as well as with respect to their rivals, will have to be developed afresh.

Conventionally, the welfare implications of Herfindahl indices, utilizing the sales revenue of firms, have been outlined under the assumption that firms operate in a homogeneous oligopoly. However, it was noted that the relevant market assumption is one of differentiated oligopoly. Hence, it is necessary to develop methods of defining Herfindahl indices at the firm level as well as at the level of individual non-price strategies of firms in such a context.

It should also be acknowledged that the firm gaining market power through price setting is a minor issue. More at stake is the prospect of non-price strategies providing the firm a larger market share which signals the emergence of market power. For all practical purposes both dimensions of market power of firms should be reckoned with. One single measure, taking account of non-price choices, of power of firms w.r.to consumers, input suppliers, possible entry of new products and/or technologies, will be superior.

It was therefore considered desirable to reverse the direction and provide a clear breakthrough from established practices to address the notion, the source and extent of market power attributable to each firm separately and to distinct non-price strategies of firms. Three advantages of this change in direction can be offered. First, the analysis of the disaggregate measures will offer useful guidelines to the management. Second, they will clearly identify the exact sources that provide the firm or the industry the market power that it has. Third, they will provide an adequate amount of information for purposes of public policy.

As a rule of thumb non-price strategies associated with the production and distribution of goods can be said to affect the market power of a firm in relation to the consumers on the market. On the other hand, variables that influence the demand side would generally have an influence on the market power of a firm through the effect on the competition between firms.

6.4. Market Power Defined

To begin with observe that in markets characterized as differentiated oligopoly the choice of the product range is itself a nonprice strategy of the firm. Thus, every firm can be deemed to have some market power based on the intrinsic value of the products they offer. This can be measured by $I_i = v_i s_i^*$, were s_i^* is determined by the consumer valuation of its products. The idea that public policy should not stifle innovative strategic choices of firms will be justifiable if the market share is limited to s_i^*. Hence, a market power index based on this dimension should be kept distinct. However, in practice, firms tend to expand beyond this based on their evaluation of the cost of informing the consumer about the value of their products. This aspect of the market power of a firm can justifiably become a target of regulatory policy. Hence, this section will highlight the measurement of market power from this perspective.

The market power of firms in the industry and that of specific non-price strategies of a firm can be developed as follows. Consider the market advantage that a firm expects vis-a-vis the consumers on the market. Clearly, it will depend on the amount of information about the value of a firm's products conveyed by the non-price strategy that the firm chooses. In general, it will depend on the expenditure E_i of the firm on non-price strategies in relation to the total spending E by all the firms in the industry.

Define $v_i = E_i / E$ as the advantage of the firm relative to the consumers in the market. (Equivalently, v_i may be the price cost margin.) This results in a market share s_i of revenue for the firm as compared to the total sales of all firms in the market. Combining these two effects results in the market power m_i of firm $i = v_i s_i$ since a fraction s_i of the total market power will accrue to firm i. Aggregating m_i over i results in the index of market power in the industry $m = \sum m_i s_i = \sum v_i s_i^2$. Redefining $t_i^2 = v_i s_i^2$ results in the familiar version $H = \sum t_i^2$. It should be recalled that this measure overcomes all the difficulties enumerated with respect to the Lerner measure as well as the Herfindhal index.

It was noted in section 4.3 that firms tend to utilize the x* up until x_1 is reached. That is, the observed market share s_i exceeds the true value s_i^* of firm i. It is, therefore, necessary to develop a specification of $s_i{}^*$ from the s_j values for all the rival firms. Consider a unit of s_i to begin with. (It can be safely assumed that the valuation of the product of firm i is reflected in s_i). In general, firm j will consider $e_j = v_j s_j / v_i s_i$ to be the extent to which firm i exceeds its true valuation per unit of s_j in its desire to obtain superior market power. The extent of over valuation by firm i in its relation to firm j will then be $e_j s_j$. Correspondingly, the average influence of the (n-1) rival firms provides the extent of excess that firm i indulges in. Hence, the true value s_i^* per unit of s_i will be $s_i^* = s_i - \sum v_j s_j^2 / v_i s_i (n-1)$. It can be argued that $I_i = v_i s_i^*$ represents the market power of firm i based on the consumer perception of the intrinsic value of its products and the elasticity of demand for its products as reflected in the market for its products. Rival firms, based on their non-price strategies, cannot reduce this. For, the consumers expressed their loyalty to the products of firm i by offering it the market share s_i^*. Consequently, the market power of firm i can be represented by $m_i = v_i s_i s_i^* = v_i s_i^2 - \sum v_j s_j^2 / (n-1)$, where the summation is over $j \neq i$. Clearly, this measure accounts for the consumer valuation of the product in the market as well as the reactions of rival firms in the industry.

Assume that firms are arranged in the decreasing order of s_i starting from the highest. If the indices m_i can be constructed sequentially there will a value M+1 of i at which $m_i < 0$. This would indicate that only M firms have market power. Their choices should be examined further to determine the requisite regulatory action.

The following observation is in order. Each measures m_i takes the threshold x* into account. It was considered necessary to allow each of the firms to have a market power commensurate with them. Hence, the sum, which takes these thresholds into account, will not contain any market power. This explains why $\sum m_i = 0$.

Note, in passing, that products like telephones, social networks on the internet and to some extent movies houses will correspond to the network effects considered above. Basically, each consumer (user) gets a value related to the size of the network. However, there is a different class of products in practice. For, there are many consumer products that provide value to the user without any reference to who else is using another unit of the same product. The appendix to this chapter will show that measures of market power developed above will be valid in that context as well.

A measure of the market power of the non-price strategy j; j = 1, 2, ..., N of firm i can be developed in an analogous fashion. Let $s_{ij} = E_{ij} / E_i$ be the share of the j th strategy in the total spending of firm i on all the non-price strategies. Then, $m_{ij} = v_i s_{ij}$ will be the indicator of the market power of the j th strategy with respect to consumers on the market. The market power of strategy j will then be $H_j = \sum m_{ij} s_{ij} = \sum v_i s_{ij}^2$, where the summation is over i for the chosen j.

Analogous to the above specification the market power of strategy j for firm i can also be specified as $m_{ij} = s_{ij}^2 - \sum s_{kj}^2 / (n-1)$, where the summation is over $k \neq i$. That is, the net market power of strategy j to firm i is obtained by subtracting the average effect of rivals on its choice. In addition, if $s_{ij} = 1$ and $s_{ik} = 0$ for all $k \neq i$ it follows that $m_{ij} = 1$ indicating maximum market power. Similarly, if $s_{ij} = 1/n$ for all j, the value of m_{ij} reduces to zero. This is a consequence of none of the strategies having any advantage relative to others. (Note that the logical equivalence of these two measures can be established as in the context of market power of firms noted above.)

Recalling the calculation regarding the firm level market power it would be useful to arrange s_{ij} in decreasing order and compute m_{ij} . It will be observed that only a few strategies would be such that $m_{ij} > 0$. Only these strategies matter in considerations of regulatory policy.

The welfare implications of the measurement at a more general level would also indicate the necessity for and the nature of regulatory limits of specific non-price choices of firms. It is pertinent to note that non-price strategies have effects over and above those bestowed upon firms by imperfect markets per se. The measures based on non-price strategies supplement the market measures. They are not meant to replace them altogether.

6.5. An Application

The application of this approach to the example of the previous chapter suggests that utilizing $v_i^{1/2} s_i$ while defining market dominance may be superior though the relevant variables do not change by very much. More obviously the ranking of strategies does differ.

1. Consider the market power in the industry. If the Herfindhal index based on market shares is utilized its value will be .2770. On the other hand, if price-cost margins at the firm level are utilized it will be .1881. The modified index indicates that the market power of the industry is .0536. It is not clear if these numbers are comparable or that their relative significance can be decoded. In other words, it is not possible to specify the sources of market power that each of these indices represents. They do not have any practical significance.

2. The firm level Lerner measures have been specified as .19,.21,.40,.02,.10, and .08 respectively. On the other hand, if the method of identifying dominance suggested in the previous chapter is utilized these market power indices will be as follows. The numbers in the brackets correspond to the indices based on the new measure proposed in this study.

	F1	F2	F3	F4	F5	F6
PR		.2500				
		(.0420)				
MS	.1629					
	(.0855)					
PCM			.1876			
			(.0480)			
SP				.1562		
				(.0022)		
MV					.1057	.0000
					(.0040)	(.0064)

Hence, different firms choose different objectives and their monopoly power is dependent on the objectives they choose. Once again it is not possible to specify the reasons why firms choose the objectives they do or their relative significance. The same type of difficulty presents itself in interpreting the results from the new index.

3.The market power that firms derive from the use of product characteristics turn out to be the following.

	F1	F2	F3	F4	F5	F6
VR	.1400	.1332	.0965	.4317		
	(.15)	(.31)	(.12)	(.27)		
CSP	.1412		.0974			
	(.33)		(.11)			
FG			.0924		.1848	.2065
			(.1)		(.47)	(.23)
ESS		.1072	.0777			
		(.15)	(.27)			
MPP	.1491	.1424				
	(.42)	(.20)				
EI			.0927		.1853	.2072
			(.12)		(.27)	(.41)
FR			.1167			
			(.43)			
SU			.7760	.3468		.1733
			(.41)	(.10)		(.20)

The following observations are pertinent. First, the market power of firms corresponds closely to the market dominance w.r.to specific choices of the firms elucidated in the previous chapter. However, it may be necessary to extend the notion of market power to three or more strategic choices at least in the context of some firms. In general, all strategies that can be characterized as satisfying the s,t properties would be useful candidates even if the number of strategies pursued by different firms vary. Second, one peculiarity is presented by firm F_4. For this firm VR has been a dominant strategy. However, it could not attract any market power. The only possible inference is that its strategic choice needs improvement to obtain market power over the rivals given that it has very little market power w.r.to the consumers on the market. On the other hand, it derives market power w.r.to the choice of FG. It would do well to improve the choices to achieve market dominance w.r.to this strategy. Third, by way of contrast, some strategies provide market power viewed from the perspective of the new index though such strategies are not dominant. Examples are MPP of F_2, VR of F_3, EI of F_5. These firms depend more on the market power in relation to consumers rather than on product strategies. It must be noted that F_3 utilizes several product strategies to consolidate its market power obtained in relation to its customers. Though it is expected that firms depend on non-price strategies only when their market power w.r.to consumers is low the evidence here does not support that viewpoint.

The following observations are pertinent. First, the market power of firms corresponds closely to the market power obtained in relation to its customers. Though it is expected that firms depend on non-price strategies only when their market power w.r.to consumers is low the evidence here does not support that viewpoint.

In addition, when the market power w.r.to consumers in the market is high (i.e., the price cost margins are high) firms tend to concentrate on a few products and consolidate their market shares. On the other hand, when the price cost margins are low firms prefer to adopt a variety of product strategies to consolidate and/or increase their market share.

The market power that firms achieve by using their non-price choices turned out to be the following

	F1	F2	F3	F4	F5	F6
BP			-			.1207
			(.0056)			(.0078)
ISR		.1230				
		(.0266)				
MO	.1440					
	(.0282)					
PD			-		.1052	
			(.0017)		(.0083)	
DU			-	.1181		-
			(.0017)	(.00009)		(.0010)
ADV		.1551				
		(.0112)				
DP				.0634		
				(.0654)		
OS			-	-	.1452	
			(.0025)	(.0016)	(.0007)	
LOC	.1205	-				
	(.0234)	(.0030)				
RS			-			.1584
			(.0152)			(.0089)
DE	.1584					
	(.0325)					

The following inferences are significant. First, observe that, as in the case of product choices, the market power of firms corresponds closely to the market dominance that they have. Though LOC for firm 1 was marked only as a s in the previous chapter it is the third largest in that column and could have been treated as a t as well. This explains the market power of firm 1. Second, firms that have high market power w.r.to consumers tend to consolidate their position by product choices in preference to non-price decisions. Perhaps the reason is that in the long run product choices, once they attract consumer loyalty, are much more difficult to dislodge. Third, as noted above, firms that have a high market power w.r.to consumers in the market tend to utilize far more non-price strategies to consolidate their market power.

Two further observations are in order. First, in the case of non-recurrent purchases like cars, TV sets and mobile phones the consumer is generally clear about the value of the product before purchase. Further, there will be few repeat purchases. The firms prefer to leave the search to the consumers. Hence, they adopt fewer non-price strategies. Consider products like daily use consumer goods and ready to wear garments. Firms are not clear about consumer loyalty for their products. Hence, they tend to emphasize many product strategies and fewer non-price strategies to consolidate their market shares rather than improve their price cost margins.

When the market power w.r.to consumers in the market is high (i.e., the price cost margins are high) firms tend to concentrate on a few products and consolidate their market shares. On the other hand, when the price cost margins are low firms prefer to adopt a variety of product strategies to consolidate and/or increase their market share.

It is possible to conceptualize the market power that a firm wishes to achieve along the lines of the calculation stated above. It can be done based on the t values marked in the last chapter. For example, consider F1. It wishes to achieve dominance w.r.to MPP and CSP. The market power that it wishes to achieve, in comparison to other strategies that it can choose from, will be .1647 for MPP and .0897 for CSP. The total market power that it wishes to achieve will then be .2544. However, it can achieve this market power only if rival firms allow it to do so. Hence, it was considered appropriate to use strategies marked as s for each firm to compute its market power. The difference will be attributable to the inefficiency of the managerial decision process which does not try to achieve dominance with respect to all the strategies that rival firms allow. (In the context of cyberspace each firm may be utilizing several non-price strategies. Some of these strategies provide market power to a firm relative its other choices. Such identification may be useful in devising regulatory policy.)

6.6. Looking Back

The important observation from this exercise is that a firm will only have market power w.r.to a few non-price characteristics. Hence, calculating the market power of the firm based on these choices alone would be justifiable. Observe that the indices were based on comparisons of the same strategy across firms. However, an equivalent procedure comparing a non-price strategy across other strategies of the same firm would be informative as well. These indices provide more viable and economically justifiable alternatives to the Herfindahl index. It will be shown in the next chapter that the usual regulatory policy arguments, listed earlier, will carry over even if this modified method is put in practice.

It can be claimed that the methods proposed here are superior to both the Lerner measure and the Herfindahl index in three ways. First, they enable identification of the market power at the level of the non-price choices that can be integrated backwards. Second, the method provides a procedure for isolating the strategies which provide positive market power to a specific firm. Third, they are much easier to justify based on welfare economics. In the next chapter it will be shown that they are also superior in the context of regulatory policy.

Note that in the analysis of this chapter the market power of the firm i was represented by $m_i = v_i\, s_i$, where v_i = price cost margin of firm i, and s_i its market share. However, profit maximization may not be the objective of the firm. Suppose it is the maximization of the market share instead. It is generally achieved at a lower price cost margin even if the total profit increases. The market share in the total revenue of all firms may be used as a measure of v_i instead. However, the closer s_i is to the market share of others the greater will be the probability of the consumer switching between products. Define $\rho_i = s_i \sum s_j / \sum s_j^2$, where the sum is over $j \neq i$. Clearly, $\rho_i = s_i\,(1\text{-}s_i) / \sum s_j^2$. Given the reactions of the rivals, the firm can retain a market share denoted by $(1 - \rho_i)\, s_i$. This measure may replace v_i. What provides the firm this share in comparison to its rivals? It may be suggested that the relative cost advantage gives the firm the advantage it has. Suppose $r_j = c_i / c_j$, where c_i = average cost of production of firm i, represents the cost advantage over firm j. Then $r_a = \sum r_j / (n\text{-}1)$, where the sum over $j \neq i$ describes the relative advantage of the rivals.

However, the cost comparisons may not be the best choice. For, a variety of choices of the firm may be at the apex of the advantage that the firm has.

Assume, for the sake of argument, that the firm under consideration targets market shares as its objective. As a result, $v_i = s_i$ may be more appropriate. What is the major strategic action that the firm utilizes to achieve this? It may be advertising intensity a_i defined as advertising expenditure per unit sales of firm i. Then, $s_i = f(a_i)$ is expected and the market power of firm i will be $m_i = \sum s_i a_i$. It is also possible to define a_i = advertising expenditure of firm i / total advertising expenditure of all firms. Assume, on the other hand, that firm i considers its relation to production workers as the critical choice to move towards the desired s_i. In such a case a_i = production workers/ total workforce, or a_i = wages per worker/ price of a unit of output sold may be appropriate. Consider the price to average cost of the firm as the major target of the firm. Suppose the firm tries to achieve this by choosing a large enough output and sales. Then $p_i/ AC_i = v_i$ and s_i may well be the choices through which it aims to achieve its objective. It is equally plausible that firms try to keep their average cost below the average of all other firms as the indicator of their advantage with respect to consumers on the market. Dynamic dominance and market power may necessitate several other choices. From a conceptual standpoint there are very many alternatives. It would not be possible to fix one of them on purely theoretical grounds. Viewed from this vantage point the measurement of the market power of a firm becomes subjective and can perhaps be chosen to justify any preconceived notion of the industry about the market power of any specific firm. It would be necessary to arrive at a theoretically justifiable specification to make an unbiased regulatory statement. $v_i = p_i/AC_i$ and s_i = market share of firm i in total sales may yet be the best compromise. But it must be kept in mind that there is no reason to view this as the only justifiable conceptualization of the market power of a firm. In the final analysis it would not be surprising if specific market power measures turn out to be better guides of managerial decision processes rather than regulatory policy.

Three further aspects of the consumers recognizing the value of a commodity require attention. First, from the viewpoint of the firm, the value of the product is only one aspect. Firms are more concerned about the quantities of the commodities they can sell. Similarly, the advertising and selling expenses do not generally matter to consumers once they bought a good. The recall value of advertisements should take over. Second, a consumer derives value from advertisements, warranties etc., only to the extent they themselves spend money and /or time examining the products.

In other words, a consumer would obtain a flow of necessary information from the stock of advertisements of the firm only to the extent they incur private spending. In addition to this the value of the product to the consumer, as is relevant to the calculation of market power, depends on the saving obtained, over and above what would have to be spent on searching for it. Such calculation of saving matters in advertisements that affect the purchase, the quantity bought and so on. Third, many consumers would simply not watch or pay attention to the advertisements if they do not wish to. Similarly, in the context of more pointed approaches to specific consumers through the internet, they will not be effective so long as the consumer is free to delete such messages. Hence, more detailed information on the impact on non-price decisions – not merely the quantity of it – would be necessary to decide their impact on the identification of value to the consumer and the possibility of repeat purchases of an equal quantity or more of it.

This opens a Pandora's box. It is not possible to arrive at a single choice as appropriate based on any objective criterion.

However, a few issues regarding the notion of market power remain. In a market where n firms produce differentiated products, even when they are substitutable, may mean that each firm has some advantages over rivals. The advantages may be w.r.to the size of fixed capital, capacity utilization, having a large market share, better organizational arrangements leading to lower costs, loyalty of consumers, workers, input suppliers and/or marketing agents. Indeed, both less than full utilization and over utilization of capacity would indicate higher than minimum average costs and lower price cost margins. It cannot be claimed that low price cost margins necessarily imply a higher elasticity of demand. In other words, a firm may have market power even if the price cost margins are the same for all and the market shares are identical for all firms. Under monopolistic conditions firms may experience near zero profits but still have significant market power. It can be concluded that the definition of market power has many dimensions and any one definition cannot reflect all the nuances. It is yet necessary to investigate and define an appropriate measure of market power.

Behavioral economics has been, of late, making inroads into understanding the psychological dimensions associated with non-price strategies and how they impact the value specification of different products and the prices the consumers are willing to pay for them. It may be expected that they will offer more quantifiable consequences of several non-price strategies.

Appendix

An Alternative Case

Assume, as in the case of many consumer products, that the value derived by the consumption of a product is exclusively related to the individual and is independent of how many others are using the same product. Let v* be the value to the consumer of a unit of the product. As before the consumer will pay a price less than or equal to v*. In the initial stages, when the product is introduced and the consumer buys it for the first time, the intrinsic value is not known. Each of the consumers may find searching for the value to be expensive; perhaps more than the value they expect to discover. Surely advertising by the firm will be far more efficacious. Let x represent the advertising intensity (share of selling expenses relative to the total advertising expenditure of the industry). It is quite reasonable to expect that the market share of revenue for the firm is $s = \alpha x$ where α is a constant. v* will be revealed when x reaches a value x* and the corresponding s* is attained. Lager values of x will not produce a value exceeding v*. Let

$C_x = Cx$ be the cost to the firm for per unit sales. It will be postulated that $Cx^* < v^*$ and there will be a x_1 such that $v^* = Cx_1$. Clearly, $x_1 = v^*/C > v^*$ since the firm would not find advertising worthwhile in the contrary case. From the viewpoint of the firm expanding s* to a higher value s_1 is feasible. In general, the observed s of the firm will be higher than s*.

As noted earlier, the market power of the firm, if it corresponds to s* should not attract regulatory action since each firm having a different s* based on x* is justified when products of firms are differentiated.

As in the previous analysis, it would be reasonable to assume that all the rival firms recognize that s chosen by a firm is higher than s*. The analytical problem is to discover s* from observed s if estimating x* and the corresponding s* is difficult. It can be argued that a rival firm j, with a market share s_j and value v_j would consider firm i to overestimate s_i^* per unit of s_j to be $(v_j s_j / v_i s_i)$ so that the total overestimation is $v_j s_j^2 / v_i s_i$. That is, every unit of s_i can be deemed to be overestimated by $\sum v_j s_j^2 / v_i s_i (n-1)$ on an average over all its rivals. It can be inferred that $v_i^* = s_i - \sum v_j s_j^2 / v_i s_i (n-1)$. The market power of firm i will therefore be $m_i = v_i s_i^2 - \sum v_j s_j^2 / (n-1)$ taking both the market power attributable to its interface with the consumers on the market and rival firms.

As before, $\sum m_i = 0$ for the simple reason that the market can be deemed to be efficient if every firm derives its advantage depending only on its s_i*. Consequently, the measure of market power developed earlier, can be deemed to be valid in this context as well.

CHAPTER 7

REGULATION

"Progress consists of unbundling the features of a social process as much as we can to maximize the human benefits while minimizing the harms." - (Pinker, 2018, p.94).

Abstract

This chapter highlights the differences between the objectives of the consumers and firms as the major disagreement in market functioning. Different aspects of necessary regulation have been identified. Various regulatory measures and their efficacy have been outlined.

7.1. Consumers vs. Firms

Economic theory generally postulates that consumers specify the prices they are willing to pay for commodities or services based on the value they perceive. They also reveal the quantities they will buy at the predetermined prices. Firms have been postulated to obtain this information and produce goods accordingly. In practice, firms have independence in choosing what information to use and which ones to discard. For, some information would not be in consonance with their profit maximizing objectives. This sows the seeds of discontent.

In fact, there has been a reversal in the direction of causation in the context of manufactured goods. More recent economic analysis therefore postulates that firms produce goods in the first instance and consumers, once they get to know their existence and value to them, express their preferences. Firms have an important role in providing consumers the information about the value of the products they bring to the market. Firms may also persuade consumers to buy their products. This tends to be important given the heterogeneity in consumer preferences for the variety of products on offer.

The emergence of the disparity between the goals of the firms and the consumers tends to be glaring. For, firms invariably choose products and processes to achieve their objectives – such as maximizing market share, profits, the share prices, reserves and surpluses, and/or the market value of the firm – in consonance with the expectations of their shareholders. On the contrary, consumers desire low prices, maximum addition to the value of the products in use, and the promptness in the delivery of goods. The goals of the two constituents are not co-terminus. The need to bridge the gap is at the apex of regulatory policy. To be sure, there is a qualitative dimension in addition to the generally acknowledged quantitative aspects that need public policy attention. The focus of this chapter will be on the quantitative dimension alone.

7.2. Market Related

At present, all regulatory action is directed to ensure that activities such as mergers and acquisitions of a firm do not increase the market power of the industry. For, it is surmised that such activities have the effect of decreasing the number of competitive firms in the industry and thereby reducing the elasticity of demand for goods.

In theory the differences in the price cost margins should have constituted the foundation to determine regulatory action. However, the market imperfection aspect, and the distortion in pricing of products associated with it, has been rarely presented in the legal debates. The legal doctrines of regulation generally consider a market to be competitive if the market share of each of the firms is the same. Similarly, any positive market power, irrespective of its magnitude, was considered as sufficient to initiate regulatory action.

The currently utilized regulatory standards, based on the market shares of revenues, can be developed as follows. The following approach of (Warren-Bolton, 1990) is useful. Consider $n\sigma^2 = \sum (s_i - s')^2$, where s' will be 1/n since $\sum s_i = 1$ in both types of product markets described above. Hence, it follows that

$$H = \sum s_i^2 = n\sigma^2 + (1/n)$$

Postulate that $s_i = 1/n$ for all i will correspond to the competitive benchmark in the industry. In such a case $\sigma^2 = 0$. Hence, $\sigma^2 > 0$ will be one aspect of the deviation from a competitive market. Similarly, the number of firms n = 4 is postulated to represent a highly concentrated market. Under these assumptions it may be noted that,

$$n\sigma^2 = H - (1/n) > 0 \text{ if } H > 1/n = .25$$

The legal literature utilizes the following guidelines:

$H > .25$ – market is highly concentrated
$.15 < H < .25$ – moderate concentration
$.01 < H < .15$ – not concentrated
$H < .01$ – Highly competitive

This procedure can only indicate that a specific industry is concentrated. However, regulatory action is operative at the level of a firm whenever the market power of a firm is positive. Firm level information is necessary to achieve implementation.

In addition, the consideration in developing these limits is only with respect to the effect of the activities of a firm on the value generated as the consumers on the market perceive it. However, in the context of markets, where different firms offer substitutable products, firms tend to develop policies so that they can have an advantage over rival firms. In addition, there will be some intrinsic differences in the market shares of firms commensurate with the value of products to the consumers. Such choices of firms will create additional market power for each firm. Consequently, it is necessary to account for both these aspects in defining regulatory limits.

The success in the market may depend on the extent to which the strategies of firms are in consonance with the value that consumers expect. Thus, there is a necessity to define the processes of providing and utilizing information about products and how it is controlled. Regulations pertaining to the market shares have become essential from a purely welfare theoretic viewpoint.

7.3. Regulating Non-Price Strategies

Gundlach and Moss (2016) suggested that the first legal case involving non-price decisions came up in 1956. It pertained to the merger of Continental Can (which produced metal containers exclusively) with Haxel Atlas Glass Company (that produced only glass containers). The courts ruled that both products were in the same relevant market though there is no cross-price elasticity. The other famous case in the 1980s was the litigation concerning the operating system of the Microsoft Corporation. Regulation concerning several other non-price aspects of the decisions of firms are known. Clearly, regulation of telecommunications – especially number portability on mobile networks, spectrum allocation to the internet, warranty standards for other durable goods, quality considerations especially as they relate to durable goods, and regulations regarding service standards, particularly in the context of electric utilities, are in place. But such regulations appear to be piecemeal and lack a welfare theoretic foundation. It is necessary to close this gap by providing an appropriate theoretical foundation.

There has never been an acknowledgment that some firms have excessive market power with respect to rival firms. This is especially significant when the market has non-cooperative rivals. A firm which has dominance over rivals can take advantage of the consumes with respect to non- price aspects, such as quality of products and services. In short, once the market reality has moved away from the competitive ideal set up by economic theory, there will be many more significant issues, other than price cost margins that need attention. Details of non-price strategies of firms, both as they affect rival firms and the consumers in their market interaction, require analysis and regulatory action. Ultimately, a market must be competitive both with respect to the consumers as well as its non-cooperative rivals. For, n firms having equal markets shares may nevertheless exhibit behavior that is not consistent with the preferences and choices of the consumers.

7.4. Differences in Objectives

In a non-cooperative market environment firms tend to accept a lower price cost margin in the interest of higher market share. For, staying ahead of rivals in terms of market shares will be in their long run interest. Non-price strategies and their role in generating the market shares of firms have yet to receive the attention they deserve.

It was noted in chapters 1, 4 and section 7.1 above that firms have several objectives in view when confronted with rivals producing differentiated products. Particular attention was drawn to the possibility that maximum profit may not be the objective of all firms. Some firms may maximize market share, others may find large scale of capital and fixed assets necessary to achieve market dominance, and yet others may maximize the goodwill of consumers with a long run view of survival. They may indeed be pursuing a variety of objectives simultaneously though with different degrees of emphasis. However, it should be clear, given the nature of competition, that each of the firms would be able to accomplish only a subset of the desired goals. For all practical purposes, the market power of any one firm may be due to the pursuit of one or more possible objectives. The differences in the choice of dominant strategies reflects the differences in the objectives pursued by firms.

Against this background, an economic theoretical formulation of regulatory policy will be presented. The effort has been to isolate the welfare inducing influences of non-price decisions and adequately account for them in the design of regulatory regimes. Further, it must be reiterated that the suggested policies would be over and above the antitrust proposals and that they do not, in anyway, supplant them.

7.5. Using Herfindahl Indices

Turning to public policy it should be devised in such a way that the advantages to the consumer are preserved while countering the deleterious effects of non-price decisions of firms. That is, public policy towards non-price choices of firms should balance the conflict between the fulfillment of consumer goals and the extent to which the interests of the firm are satisfied. This issue can be outlined as follows.

The value of $x_1 > x^*$ and $Vx^* > Cx$ for $x^* < x < x_1$, alluded to in an earlier chapter, indicate that the consumer has something to gain by the firm increasing x to x_1. Further, trying to reduce x to x^* by increasing the cost implied by the non-price strategy will reduce the gains to the consumer. Both these features suggest that regulatory action need not be contemplated unless x_1 is exceeded. It has been increasingly obvious that the value increasing advantages that non-price strategies offer to consumers would necessitate modifications of the regulatory limits.

A few more observations will be necessary to fully appreciate the need for further considerations. First, aggregate measures of market power do not convey any information about the individual non-price choices that contribute to it. It is quite clear from the earlier chapters that in markets with differentiated products the emphasis must be on the market power of individual firms and their non-price choices. It is therefore necessary to move away from measures of aggregate market power and concentrate on the strategies that provide the firm its market dominance. The analysis should supplement the quantitative magnitude of price decisions and market shares with the choice of objectives, product line as well as non-price strategies that offer useful information. Second, a careful perusal indicates that some firms, not everyone in the industry, will account for noticeable market power. Similarly, a few strategies of firms have the major role in explaining the market power. It is necessary to track them for any further action. In the final analysis, regulatory limits must consider a level playing field for each firm based on consumer valuation. Differences between firms persist and firms will have advantages relative to rivals based purely on the value of their products about which the consumers are convinced.

The integration of the interaction of the firm with the consumers on the market with the power derived from between firm competition does suggest an improvement. However, neither of these have been defined satisfactorily when some firms in the market pursue objectives other than profit maximization. Quantitative specification of the extent of regulatory action is rarely attempted.

It is necessary to identify the industries, the firms, and/or their specific non-price strategies that require regulatory attention. Some information about this aspect can be gleaned from the measures of market power developed earlier.

In the context of cyberspace it was noted that regulatory action directed to firms would not be adequate. It would be necessary to modify the expectations of the users as well. Such a distinction may apply to other industries as well at least with respect to certain non-price choices.

7.6. Regulatory Constraints

The following conventions will be adopted for the convenience of simplicity and uniformity of notations. Normally s_i would have represented the market share of the revenue of a firm in the total revenue of all the firms in the industry. However, given the modification in the definition of market power let s_i represent $v_i^{1/2} s_i / \sum v_i^{1/2} s_i$ as defined in the previous chapter. This characterization preserves the properties of s_i normally expected.

While interpreting the results note that s_i , the way it was defined, depends on v_i as well as the characteristics of rival firms. The regulatory standards will therefore depend on industry and firm specific details rather than uniform application.

The following development related to non-price strategies is analogous to the presentation in section 7.2 above but distinctly different. As noted in the previous chapter they have been developed after taking the welfare improving dimensions of non-price strategies into account. Consider the market share s_i of any of the non-price choices. Let s_m be the minimum among s_i over i = 1, 2, ..., n. Define $H = \sum s_i^2$, were the summation is over the rest of the i = 1, 2, ..., n. Observe that writing

$$s_i^{**} = s_i / (1 - s_m) \text{ implies } \sum s_i^{**} = 1. \text{ Let}$$
$$\sigma^2 = \sum\{s_i^{**} - (1/n-1)\}^2$$
$$= \sum s_i^{**2} - 1/(n-1) = H/(1 - s_m)^2 - 1/(n-1)$$

Consequently, $H = 1/3\ (1 - s_m)^2$ if $\sigma^2 = 0$ and n = 4. Suppose $s_m = .25$. Then, H = .1875. The inference, analogous to the earlier case, will be that the firms in the market derive excessive market power if H > .1875. Other limits can be developed analogously.

The most crucial aspect in devising regulatory standards is that a single guideline will not be suitable in all contexts. Instead, accounting for the positive effects of the corresponding non-price strategy using s_m for the industry under consideration is warranted. This recognition is the strength of the proposed method.

As noted above investigating the market power of individual firms is necessary to conceptualize regulatory policies. Consider the market power of firm i, viz.,

$$m_i = s_i^2 - \sum s_j^2 / (n-1)$$

Note that $\sum s_j = (1-s_i)$. Defining σ^2 as before note that $\sum s_j^2 / (1-s_i)^2 = \sigma^2 + 1/(n-1)$. Therefore,

$$\sum s_j^2 = (1 - s_i)^{2/}(n-1).$$

Consequently, $m_i > 0$ if $s_i^2 > (1 - s_i)^{2}/ (n-1)^{2}$. That is, $ns_i > 1$. It follows that firm i has market power if $s_i > .25$ when n = 4. It is essential to recall that defined in this fashion the limits depend on the v_i in addition to the market shares of firms.

Consider the market power of firm j w.r.to the characteristic i. It was defined as

$m_{ij} = s_{ij}^2 - \sum s_{ik}^2 / (n-1)$, where the summation is over $k \neq j$. Observe that $\sum s_k = 1 - s_{ij}$.

Define

$s_{ik}^* = s_{ik} / (1 - s_{ij})$ for $k \neq j = 1, 2, ..., n$. Obviously, $H^* = \sum s_{ik}^{*2} = H / (1 - s_{ij})^2$, where $H = \sum s_{ik}^{*2}$. Similarly, define

$$\sigma^2 = \sum\{s_{ik} - (1-s_{ij})/(n-1)\}^2 = H - (1 - s_{ij})^2/(n-1)$$

Consider

$$m_{ij} = s_{ij}^2 - \sum s_{ik}^2 / (n-1) = s_j^2 - \{\sigma^2 + (1 - s_{ij})^2/(n-1)\}/(n-1)$$

Suppose $\sigma^2 = 0$. This would indicate that none of the remaining firms has any market power w.r.to the non-price strategy j. Clearly, $m_{ij} > 0$ if $s_{ij}^2 - (1 - s_{ij})^2 / (n-1)^2 > 0$. That is, $ns_{ij} > 1$.

The following inference is obvious. If $n = 4$, then $s_{ij} > .25$ indicates that the firm i has market power with respect to strategy j. In other words, regulatory guidelines developed earlier will be valid even in this context. Note that small values of n and consequently low η values should correspondingly have lower $s_{i.}$. That is, a firm should be deemed to have excessive market power if s_i is large. This is essentially the spirit of this regulatory limit.

Several observations are in order. First, considerations of regulation must acknowledge that they should apply to individual firms rather than the totality of the market in the new environment. For, claiming that a firm's actions will have a bearing on its market power necessitates its being the essential basis for regulation. (In the rest of the chapter the s_i will be the observed market share rather than the modification considered in the above argument.) In earlier work while defining the legal limits of high concentration in a market it was noted that $s_i = 1/n$ for all i will be considered as the definition of a competitive market. As a result, defining $\sigma^2 = \sum (s_i - 1/n)^2$ and $\sigma^2 > 0$ implying the existence of market power was accepted as the starting point. In the context of an industry producing differentiated products it is necessary to acknowledge that each firm will have a different s_i^* based on the intrinsic value of its product. The market can be deemed to be in equilibrium if and only if $s_i = s_i^*$ for all i. Such an equilibrium should be the benchmark for defining a competitive configuration in the market setting under consideration. The definition of σ^2 for regulatory considerations should be $\sigma^2 = (s_i - s_i^*)^2$.

The following results should be noted. First, the s_i^*, even if it cannot be estimated directly, has been shown to be equal to $s_i - \sum v_j s_j^2 / v_i s_i (n-1)$ where the summation is over $j \neq i$. In general, the observed value of s_i will exceed s_i^*. Hence, $\sum v_j s_j^2 \geq 0$ for all values of i. Writing

$\sum v_j s_j^2 = \sum_1 v_j s_j^2 - v_i s_i^2$ where $\sum_1$ is over all i, it can be verified that this necessitates $s_i > [\sum_1 v_j s_j^2 / nv_i]^{1/2}$. Second, $s_i^* \geq 0$ implies that $s_i > [\sum_1 v_j s_j^2$

$/nv_i]^{1/2}$. Hence, unlike in the above competitive assumption it must be acknowledged that the legal limit on s_i will depend on v_i. Third, note that $s_i^* = s_i - \sum v_j s_j^2 / v_i s_i (n-1)$. Hence $(n-1) v_i s_i s_i^* = n v_i s_i^2 - \sum v_i s_i^2 > 0$ for all s_i, $s_i^* > 0$ indicating thereby that $s_i > [\sum_1 v_j s_j^2 /nv_i]^{1/2}$. In sum, it must be acknowledged that the regulatory limits defined by the new method would require, and be consistent with, the market equilibrium in which $s_i = s_i^*$ for all i based on the intrinsic value of the products.

The regulatory limits, based on the new market power index, calculated for the example detailed in the earlier chapters, are as follows. The s_{ij} values in the brackets make the interpretation of the limits easier.

In general, the significance of market power being positive follows the patterns detailed by dominant strategies. However, as noted in the previous chapter F_4 has market dominance w.r.to VR but does not have market power > 0. Similarly, F_1,F_2 and F_5 indicate $m_{ij} > 0$ w.r.to VR, ESS and SU respectively though market dominance is not indicated. It can be verified that the corresponding s_{ij} is the next largest in the corresponding columns and thus indicates dominance if three strategies are accounted for. F_3 provides a different kind of exception. The strategy of this firm is to consolidate its market power w.r.to consumers in the market by utilizing a variety of product decisions.

Consider the market power based on the non-price strategies of firms. The following results emerge.

Non-Price Decisions

	F1	F2	F3	F4	F5	F6
BP			.0935			.0167
			(.15)			(.37)
ISR		.1410				
		(.37)				
MO	.1489					
	(.40)					
PD		.1332	.0959		.1916	
		(.15)	(.13)		(.35)	
DU			.0757	.3555		.1778
			(.10)	(.37)		(.23)
ADV		.1481	.1074		.2147	
		(.40)	(.15)		(.25)	
DP			.1195			
			(.41)			
OS		.1118	.811	.3621		
		(.15)	(.1)	(.40)		
LOC	.1498		.1032	.1032		
	(.37)		(.15)	(.15)		
RS		.1425	.1032			.2377
		(.16)	(.22)			(.42)
DE	.1362					
	(.42)					

It is important to note that F_3 also utilizes several non-price strategies in its attempts to consolidate its market power just as it is using product strategies. For all the firms in the example the glaring disparities are, of course, in the choice of dominant strategies.

The market power of the individual strategies of a firm towards their contribution to its market power can also be examined without any basic analytical changes.

7.7. Regulatory Instruments

It would be useful to develop a simple analytical framework to fold in all the possible regulatory measures together.

Recall that the primary purpose of non-price strategies is to help the consumer in recognizing the intrinsic value of a product made available on the market. However, the firm cannot influence the valuation beyond the value experienced by the consumer. Let x denote the market share of a non-price strategy. Postulate that the valuation revealed by the consumer is $V(x) = Vx$. However, as x increases the consumer evaluates the value of the product. Let its full value be revealed when $x = x^*$. That is, $V^* = Vx^*$. Thereafter the value will remain constant at V^*.

Let the costs to the firm, of utilizing the non-price strategy, be $C = Cx$. It can be assumed that $V > C$. For, otherwise, it is not possible for the advertisers to gain. There exists a x_1 at which $C = V^*$. It is given by $x_1 = V^*/C$. Normally this will be greater that x^*.

The consumers do not want x to be greater than x^*. However, the firm will generally expand at least to x_1 for two reasons. First, a higher profit can be obtained at the higher market share even if the profit per unit sold decreases. Second, in a non-cooperative market environment it is essential that the firm does not allow rivals to cut into its market in its long run interest. Such a choice of $x > x_1$ is usually the basic reason for regulatory action.

While $x^* < x < x_1$, the consumers do derive an additional value. If it accrues entirely to the consumers there will be no justification for regulatory action. However, there can be an increase in profits of the firm for the simple reason that the firm charges a price commensurate with V^*. This may attract regulatory action.

Since the firms generally include the costs of administering the non-price strategies in the cost of goods sold the profits will also be affected. This, in turn, reduces the profit taxes paid. Hence, one of the regulatory measures would be to limit the write-off of costs. Strictly, it should correspond to x^* at which the market power of the firm is reduced to zero. Operationally the minimum market share attained by firms in the market should be subtracted from all others to account for the welfare increasing effects of non-price strategies.

In the context of cyberspace it was noted that regulatory action directed to firms would not be adequate. It would be necessary to modify the expectations of the users as well. (At least with respect to certain non-price choices such a distinction may apply to other industries as well.)

These results have been achieved by reinterpreting some conventional notions from a contemporary perspective. The interpretation of market power after accounting for the welfare increasing property of the decisions of firms was the small thing that gave rise to the fundamental insights presented in this study.

7.8. Further Considerations

The framework of analysis has not been designed to cover all the necessary aspects of regulation. Some aspects that require further attention may now be stated.

In the context of franchises and subsidiaries in other locations the parent firm utilizes them to reduce its investments though they receive a share of profits. This reduces their market share but it is difficult to claim that their market power is reduced. The regulatory action necessarily depends on the assessment of value addition to consumers.

Some strategies of expansion, based on economies of scale and/scope, will reduce the costs of production. In such a case x^* will be larger. But the above argument still holds. The context of inventory policy, warehousing and distribution arrangements will also belong to this category.

Regulatory policy may be needed if spending on non-price choices has been such as to create barriers to entry, restrict supplies to consumers or suppliers of inputs to firms. The measures of dominance and market power may be indicators but cannot be said to provide adequate proof.

Firms tend to be innovative in their choices of non-price strategies. In general, if the regulator tries to curb one type of expenditure firms will resort to another choice. It may, therefore, be suggested that the total expenditure on non-price strategies should be the target of the regulator. The necessary tools to recognize the excessive use of the totality of non-price strategies need further study.

CHAPTER 8

CYBERSPACE REGULATION

"Scientists are increasingly seeing ... bursts of activity in a larger system, intelligible only when studied in the context of many examples of the same phenomenon. They are turning their attention to how and why the parts of it fit together and to rules that govern interconnection and coherence." - (Christakis and Fowler, 2009, p.304).

Abstract

The apps on the internet present a different type of regulatory concern. It is basically the individuals who post information that create the congestion and externalities. However, the apps do not ask them to specify the information that can be made available to others and the information they wish to keep private. Regulatory action directed to individuals should make them responsible to spell out the limits, charge membership fees and fees for specific information posted on the app. The apps should be expected to modify their search engines. These and other regulatory policies have been presented.

8.1. The Issues

It is well known that Google, Facebook, Airbnb and many other corporations started by catering to limited uses of a small group of individuals. They have grown into large corporations based on network effects mostly financed by advertising revenues. Almost all of us recognize that we cannot achieve similar network effects by pursuing the activities outside these apps. As Young (2012) put it,

"no matter how unhappy you might be with how Facebook deals with your privacy, leaving Facebook starts to feel like pushing yourself out to the sea."
- (Young, 2012, 106)

However, there is an increasing concern about issues of privacy of information and abuse of market power by such corporations. Many studies are suggesting that they need to be regulated. Young (2012) expressed it succinctly:

> "No matter how information is disclosed, we still need rules that govern what a company can do with an individual's information, and these restrictions ought not to be the sort of a thing a user waives in the terms of service agreements." - (Young, 2012, 180)

Alleman et al (2019) and Neuman (2019) provided a compelling case for legal restrictions on such firms.

The essential problem can be traced to the conflict between the objectives of the users and the service providers. What matters from the individual viewpoint is the intrinsic value of information that grows with network effects. On the other hand, from the viewpoint of the corporations, market dominance - defined mostly by the size of its network, increased (advertising) revenues and profits - come into reckoning. These two requirements complement each other to an extent. However, there is a growing feeling that the networks reached a point where the goals of the individuals and the apps are in conflict. The primary contention is that networks are transmitting information provided by individuals to the corporations that provide them finances. They, in turn, use the information against the same individuals who provided the information (primarily in the form of attempts to sell their products).

Two other aspects need mention. First, it should be noted that the information overload, containing unwanted information, may in fact be partly due to services of apps being free. In practice, each of us have limits on the nature of information we need and the quantum of information thereof. As a result, problems arise since more than necessary information is being stored on the apps. Indeed, the costs of processing the high volume of information, even if we wish to have it, can be prohibitive. For all practical purposes it is necessary for individuals to know their limits and spell them out to the apps. Second, from the viewpoint of the firms the advertisers pay most of their costs. That entices the apps to provide more information in the interest of their profit potential. Conceptually, limiting the advertising revenues will eventually bring the network sizes to the proportions that we consider desirable. Clearly, this suggests a shift of regulatory activity to the firms that sponsor the advertisements. It is necessary to decide the level at which these regulations should be targeted.

The opponents who argue against regulatory action seem to dominate. They offer four reasons. First, the decisions of these firms usually offer useful (value increasing) information to the individuals in their quest to improve their welfare. Second, their influence on market power is rather negligible (a proof has not been forthcoming). Third, the market power advantages are purely transitory in nature and the operation of many competing apps will eventually eliminate them (recent experiences do not corroborate this viewpoint). Fourth, any regulatory policies directed towards their strategies will stifle innovation apart from inhibiting possible welfare gains. Quite the contrary, it will be shown in what follows that innovative activities will flourish if regulatory policies are efficacious.

Against this background the rest of the chapter is organized as follows. Section 2 briefly recalls the financing of the apps by advertisements of firms. For all practical purposes this is a source of revenue for the apps. The boundaries of the industry will be defined using the quantum of advertisements. Similarly, this section provides brief details of the products that the apps provide. Section 3 outlines the emergence of market power utilizing the needs of the subscribers in view. Section 4 provides methods of measuring market dominance corresponding to products of each firm, the firm, and the industry. These indices will indicate the details of the targets that regulatory policy should consider. Section 5 provides specifics of the regulatory limits in legal practice. Section 6 details the likely instruments of regulatory policy. Clearly, they will be classified as those relating to the users themselves, the apps and the firms that are providing the advertisements. In the ultimate analysis the purpose of regulatory policy is to provide a level playing field to the apps and make sure that they keep the welfare of the subscribers, as the users perceive it, in view. Section 7 describes how some of the regulatory measures deliver the objectives for which they have been set up. Section 8 provides an overview.

8.2. Characterizing industry

It is necessary to clarify the concept of the industry to which the apps belong. For, on the face of it an app like Facebook does not seem to have any rivals. In particular, the nature of services they provide do not have an equivalent in any other apps. However, the dependence of the apps, for the advertising revenues of the same or similar firms, indicates that they are competitive in that market. Several of the apps may have the same subscribers as well. This, as well as the difficulty in getting information about the number of subscribers, makes it difficult to use the number of subscribers as an indicator of the size of an app. It should also be recognized that different apps will have different number of individuals on their network. This will indicate the differences in the advertising revenues that they can attract. That is, the number of subscribers on the app will be strongly correlated with the advertisement revenues that the app receives. In sum, the convenience of obtaining information about advertising revenues tips the scales in favor of using that as a desideratum.

The subscribers will consider the information stored as a proxy for the value that they obtain from the services of the app. Similarly, the advertisement revenue for the app will be a good enough proxy for the costs to the subscriber. Keeping this in view the size of a firm can be defined as the megabytes or giga bytes of information stored on the central servers of the app.

Turning to the products or services offered by the apps it would be practical to classify them in the following way: Personal, professional, entertainment and music, travel, and leisure and political. The groups can be subdivided based on the needs of the analysis and the availability of data. The regulatory proposals will differ from one type of service to the other.

The issues for regulatory policy will be information overload, privacy of information, abuse of market power and barriers to entry, and the prices charged for advertised products. The available regulatory policies may be directed towards the subscribers, the apps and/or the advertising firms as the case warrants.

8.3. Number of subscribers

Even if the market power measure cannot be calculated w.r.to the number of subscribers the following analysis can provide guidelines about the sources of market power and the types of regulatory measures that can be used in practice.

Consider the context of an app that has n individuals signed into it. When n is small the individuals in the group will necessarily know each other. Consider the option of increasing n. Let V_n be the value to the individual of the larger network. It can be represented by $V_n = Vn$ where V is a constant. This corresponds to the empirical intuition that the availability of many individuals on the network increases the value of the information sought (network effect).

The option for individuals is to search and trace the other individuals with whom they want contacts. Assume that the cost of search is $S = - S_0 +$

Sn. There will be no need for search until n reaches a positive value. Further, it is being posited that the costs of search will increase significantly if the individuals try to establish several contacts on their own. The individual will stop searching when the S_n associated with n exceeds the value V_n. Such an n is given by $n_a = S_0/ (S - V)$. It is natural to assume that $S > V$. There will be no advantage for the individual to incur search costs if $n > n_a$. In the initial stages, where there is not enough activity for apps to find it economical, they will allow subscribers to search for the value of the product. Only after a critical mass is considered possible will the apps begin to offer their services and begin signaling about the advantages of membership in them. For, firms try to avoid the cost of signaling, to the extent possible, in their quest to maximize profits.

Now suppose the firm chooses to signal the value of its offering for which $n > n_a$. As the operations expand further the apps need to depend on advertising to cover the costs of their installing central servers, developing the search engines and maintaining them to ensure optimum delivery of the promised services. Let the signaling cost be $I_n = In$. It must be acknowledged that individuals have limits on the amount of information they can process or utilize. Similarly, the apps have limits on the total number of bytes of information that they can process given the storage capacity on its central servers and their search algorithms. As a result, it should be expected that when individuals would find that the information available is no longer of any additional value for the subscribers when their number exceeds a limit. Ill effects of being a subscriber will be experienced if the app persists on increasing the number of subscribers beyond this point. The excess represented by this occurrence will be a measure of the market power of the app vis-a-vis its subscribers.

Let n* be the number of subscribers that reflect the limit. In such a case $V(n) = Vn^*$ for $n^* \leq n \leq m$. However, the app may have resources to cater to $n_1 > n^*$ of subscribers. Similarly, the limit on the total service they can offer will be T (say). This can be represented in the following equation:

$$Vmn^* - Vn^{*2}/2 = T$$

Accordingly, the limit on n* will be determined by T, m and V. This can be detailed as follows. Suppose there is a ceteris paribus increase in m. Since the app is catering to a larger number of subscribers the information load increases and n* will decrease. This can be verified by noting that $dn^*/dm = n^*/(n^* - m) < 0$ since $m > n^*$. Let V increase instead. Each subscriber requires more information on the app. As a result, the n* at which all the necessary information can be made available increases. This is reflected in

$$dn^*/dV = n^* (2m - n^*) / 2Vn^* > 0$$

On the other hand, an increase in T indicates an increase in the capacity of the app. Hence, it can be expected that a larger number of subscribers can be taken care of. n* will increase. For, observe that

$$dn^*/dT = 1/ V(m - n^*) > 0.$$

It is equally significant to note that advertisers would wish to increase n beyond n*. Hence, n_1 will be such that $Vn^* = In_1$. Such a $n_1 > n^*$ since V > I. Will the subscribers accept the network expansion? First, the subscribers are getting the maximum value they expect. They would not be averse to obtaining some extra information so long as V(n) > I(n). Second, if some taxes are imposed to reduce n there will be a reduction in value to the subscribers beyond the limit specified above. Hence, $n_1 > n^*$ should not be considered as providing market power to the app.

The foregoing analysis clearly demonstrates the value of being a member of a network, the possibility of the individual getting the advantages of the network effect at no cost most of the time, the possibility that the apps would try to utilize excessive advertising (which, in any case, is not a cost to it) not commensurate with the value increase of the number of individuals on the network, and the imperative for the apps to utilize innovative ideas of finance to avoid regulatory action.

This conceptualization clearly defines the approach to the market power of the app relative to the subscribers. The apps market power w.r.to rival apps will be developed in the next section so that an overall market power index can be constructed.

For purposes of the rest of the analysis it should be recognized that the above description considers the number of individuals on each network. The differences between the apps may also be due to the nature of the service provided, the finances that the network can garner and the technical constraints if any. The number of subscribers on the network being excessive as well as the inefficient use of advertising for finances will become issues for regulatory policy.

8.4. Market Power

The first important question relates to the market power of the different apps and the variety of applications of each app. For, in the ultimate analysis, different instruments of control may have to be applied to different applications after determining the relative market power of specific applications.

As noted earlier there are two sources of market power for any app. First, its relationship with the subscribers and the value delivered to them. The number of subscribers on the network is a useful approximation. Second, its position vis-a-vis rival apps in the industry. The advertising revenues of the apps may be the best index of this relative position. A general index of market power can be developed by using the market value of the services of the apps to the users and the share of advertising revenues that the app obtains.

Let v_i represent the number of bytes of information on app i; i = 1, 2, ..., n, relative to the advertising revenues that the app receives. Denote by s_i the ratio of advertisement revenues of app i relative to the total of all other apps. Then, $v_i s_i$ will signify the market power m_i of app i. The market power of the industry will then be

$$H = \sum m_i s_i = \sum v_i s_i^2$$

Note that it is composed of an advantage in the market for information and that achieved in relation to other apps. The weights assigned are the market shares of the apps in advertising revenues since they represent the intensity of the value generated.

One important observation is in order. As noted in section 8.2, the apps try to expand their membership, and consequently the information stored, up until the market share reaches n_1. The observed v_i is an overestimate of the true value of the app to the subscribers. This must be accounted for while constructing the market power indices. However, it is operationally not possible to measure this range n^* to n_1. Hence, an equivalent measure will be proposed.

Define

m_i = market power of firm i
$= s_i^2 - \sum s_j^2 / (n-1)$, where the sum is over $j \neq i$.

The equivalence of this to the measure proposed above can be established as follows. To begin with observe that v_i is strictly related to the number of subscribers and the information they store. The other apps recognize that app i views the excess as a defensive mechanism against possible intrusion by rival apps. In general, app j will consider $e_j = s_j / s_i$ as the extent to which app i goes beyond the value maximum per subscriber on j in the interest of maintaining its competitive position. Correspondingly, the average influence of the rivals on app i will be

$\sum s_j (s_j/s_i) / (n - 1)$. Hence, the true valuation v_i per subscriber on app i will be

$v_i = s_i - \sum (s_j^2 / s_i) / (n-1)$

It follows that the market power of app i will be

$m_i = v_i\, s_i = s_i^2 - \sum s_j^2 / (n-1)$

Clearly this measure accounts for the subscriber valuation of the app in relation with them as well as the reactions of rival apps in the industry.

The following observation is in order. Assume that s_j are arranged in decreasing order. There will be some value n** of i at which $m_i < 0$. (n**-1) apps can then be said to have market dominance in the industry. The others do not have any market power. Hence, only the first (n** - 1) apps attract regulatory action.

App i also derives its market power from the concentration of its use in different types of applications. Let s_{ij} represents the share of information corresponding to each type of use. Application j provides app i market power equivalent to $v_i\, s_{ij}$. The market power of app i can be developed by aggregating over j. It results in

$H_i = \sum v_i\, s_{ij}^2$

The market power of application j for app i can be equivalently represented by

$m_{ij} = s_{ij}^{\ 2} - \sum s_{ik}^2 / (N-1)$

where N is the number of applications on app i and the summation is over all other applications on app i.

Two observations are important. First, assume that s_j are arranged in decreasing order. There will be some value N* of j at which $m_j < 0$. (N*-1) applications can then indicate dominance for app i. The others do not have any market power. Hence, only the first (N* - 1) applications attract regulatory action. Second, some of the (N* - 1) applications may not attract regulatory action because the advantages to the subscribers are not significantly different from the advertisement revenues they attract.

Clearly, the market power of app i, its dominance over other apps as well as the dominance of application j over application k for the same i will have implications for targeting regulatory policy.

8.5. Regulatory Limits

The following presentation will highlight the assumptions under which the regulatory standards in vogue have been obtained. Return to the definition of market power in the industry, viz.,

$$m = \sum v_i s_i^2$$

The following transformation will simplify the presentation. Define

$t_i = v_i^{1/2} s_i / \sum v_i^{1/2} s_i$. The Herfindahl index of market power of the industry is $H = \sum t_i^2$, and
$\sigma^2 = \sum (t_i - 1/n)^2$.

The legal rules also assume the following: (1) Level playing field in the industry (and consequently its competitiveness) implies $t_i = 1/n$, for all i , (2) $n < 4$ indicates extreme concentration in the market, and (3) $\sigma^2 > 0$ indicates the existence of market power.

Observe that

$\sigma^2 = H - 1/n$. Consequently, if $n = 4$ the value of H will be .25. It follows that $H > .25$ signals extreme market power.

The legal literature utilizes the following guidelines:

$H > .25$ – market is highly concentrated
$.15 < H < .25$ – moderate concentration
$.01 < H < .15$ – not concentrated
$H < .01$ – Highly competitive

The important observation is that when defined in terms of t_i^2 they will depend on v_i as well. The application of market shares s_i in regulatory practice would require making proper changes in the above guidelines.

Let $t_i^* = t_i /(1-t_i)$. Maintaining the assumptions presented above it can be verified that app i can be said to have market power if $t_i^* > 1/ (n-1)$. This reduces to $nt_i > 1$.

Similar results can be developed for the disaggregate measures as well. These measures indicate the specific directions in which regulatory policy should be developed. The specific regulatory measures will depend on the nature of the application.

8.6. Regulatory Policies

The adverse effects of information on the cyberspace may be revealed by the subscribers themselves. However, it is the result of the interaction between the subscribers, the apps and the firms providing advertising revenues to the apps. Regulatory action may be directed to any or all of them. These will be detailed in the following.

Suppose currently the app is accepting n individuals. The value to them is Vn. The app is receiving In by way of advertisements. There are two options in such a setting. First, suppose a subscriber fee of F per person is set up such that $(V - F)\, n < In$. The subscribers will find the remaining value insufficient when they eventually pay higher prices for the advertisements. They will voluntarily withdraw forcing a reduction in the size of the network and the advertisers will also withdraw correspondingly. Second, the app is leaving $Vn - In$ as value added to the members. Now suppose the members say that $n^* < n$ alone is acceptable. The app is losing $I\,(n - n^*)$. To make it accept n^* the members must pay $F_m = I\,(n - n^*)/n^*$ per member. If they pay $F_M = V - I$ it would be better. But this is the maximum that each member would be willing to pay. The F set up by the regulator (implying sharing of the value generated) may be a compromise between the two. n^* would materialize only if the regulator sets that limit on membership and ask the members to pay the corresponding F. Both these regulatory clauses and monitoring would be necessary to ensure compliance.

Expecting the user of an app to pay a fee for joining and receiving service is one of the options. Notice that when the app receives revenues in the form of advertising it writes them off against costs of maintaining the app and providing the service. It has lowered its liability to corporate taxes.

Three options are discernible. First, expect the app to pay a portion of the advertising revenue as tax (this is akin to GST on revenues). Second, impose a higher profit tax rate in the form of a congestion tax. Third, a tax proportional to the rate of return out of advertising revenues can be expected. A somewhat more detailed analysis alone will suggest the optimal regulatory policy to reduce and/or eliminate the unwanted congestion effects of the apps.

Consider the subscribers to begin with. They will compare the gain in value to them, of remaining on the network, with the possible harm that they encounter when they recognize that their information is compromised. When the losses exceed the gains, they are likely to withdraw at least w.r.to some applications that generate large losses. The regulators may assist the process by expecting the apps to charge a subscription rate or the entry to the app as well as utilizing different rates for applications. Though the volumes will be reduced the abuses may continue unless the apps restructure their search engines and the use of specific information on their network. Essentially, the regulator should ensure that the app provides the specification of the exceptions of usage of their data to the subscribers and adhere to it in its dissemination. If this involves an extra cost to the app, not a technical impossibility of rewriting algorithms, it would be just as well that the subscriber is expected to bear the cost by way of user charges.

The apps are accepting an unlimited number of subscribers in the interest of attracting more advertisers and correspondingly their profits. Two other regulatory actions can be directed to them. First, the regulator may charge a tax per unit of advertising revenues received (analogous to GST). Second, the apps will tend to write off their costs when paying profit taxes. However, the advertising firms already claimed a credit for it in their accounts. Hence, it may be necessary to devise a mechanism to avoid this duplicate deduction. The expansion of the central servers has been a problem. Hence, investments in such devices, when taxed in a suitable manner, will reduce the volume of information on the app. It is for the subscribers to weigh the disadvantages and initiate appropriate action if it involves a loss in the value of information. There is a possibility that the apps would use innovative ways to avoid regulation along a certain dimension. Regulatory capture, given the immense financial power of the apps, cannot be ruled out either.

Turn to the advertisers. They do not have any direct way of causing the congestion. However, to the extent the apps depend on their spending on advertisements they do influence the quantity of information and its mode of usage. The advertisers may retract if the regulations of the apps have the desired effects. The misuse of specific application information can be contained if the apps can be directed to provide freedom to the subscribers in specifying what information can be transmitted and to whom.

The overall information on the apps will reduce but whatever is put on the network will be utilized to the satisfaction of the subscriber. The resulting flow of information may be superior to not having the apps.

8.7. Moving Forward

The basic conclusion of this chapter is that both the subscribers and the apps themselves are responsible for the problems on cyberspace. Accordingly, it would be necessary for them to make the necessary adjustments. Regulation will become mandatory if this does not come about. The possibility that some unwanted information persists on the network cannot be eliminated but minimized.

CHAPTER 9

MANAGERIAL IMPLICATIONS

"The ideas of economists and political philosophers, both when they are right and when they are wrong, are more powerful than is commonly understood. Indeed, the world is ruled by little else." – (Keynes, 1936, 383)

Abstract

Firms utilize non-price strategies to enable consumers to evaluate the intrinsic value of their products relative to those of rivals. This process enables them to achieve a market share commensurate with such valuation. However, in practice, some firms lack the managerial acumen or do not have adequate resources to sustain them over time at the desired level. In economic terms the cost of revealing the value may exceed the value so generated. Such firms will not have market dominance or market power. However efficient the managerial process may be, external conditions, either related to consumer valuation or the reactions of rival firms, may inhibit a firm from achieving market dominance. These and other details will be presented since they are as important as the market dominance that a firm achieves in practice.

9.1. The Events

The first recognition, concerning markets where differentiated products are sold relates to each firm acknowledging that its product related and non-price decisions are necessary to inform consumers of the value of their products. This is certainly more efficient and economical to leaving the search process to individual consumers. Second, though the market conditions (especially the elasticity of demand) are largely exogenous to the decision making of the firm it is natural to seek market dominance through its action to the extent it can. For, its non-price choices can and do alter the positions of the demand curves and hence the market share. Third, when firms utilize more than the minimum necessary levels to garner some market power the regulatory process is activated. This, in its turn, requires the management to identify and implement innovative non-price decisions to circumvent regulatory action as far as possible. These considerations suggest that a study of market dominance and market power will have implications for designing efficient managerial practices.

Rao (2017) observed that

> "In general, firms that offer products with a stable market share are inward looking to ensure adequate production and supplies. Similarly, they make their own arrangements to maintain their supplies to the market. On the other hand, firms seeking transient advantage are outward oriented. They place greater emphasis on choosing products that can be easily integrated into their product line, advertise sufficiently to inform the consumers of their new products, and place emphasis on delivering products to consumers at places where they want them."– (Rao, 2017, 9)

However, as Rao (2017, 10-11) argued, assuming the centrality of the product line choice and taking it for granted that all other managerial practices will be in accordance with them may not be justified. Instead, firms must adopt various other non-price policies to differentiate themselves from rivals so that their market dominance is not eroded. In other words, the actual strategic choices go well beyond what is necessary to inform the consumers of the value of their products.

The recognition that the managerial decision process may lead to market power would also suggest to the firm that it is necessary to evaluate their resource base and competence of the organizational details to sustain it or improve it. In short, it should be possible to indicate the circumstances that led the management of firms to either depend on market conditions or look inward. Any study of market dominance and market power should be able to disentangle their role in the dynamic management process and not merely inform regulators that their intervention is necessary.

To decode the objectives of the firm based on market dominance per se would be difficult. In general, there are several tradeoffs between the market value of the firm, profits, stability of long run markets, and loyalties of consumers, workers and so on. Rao and Rastogi (1997) examined some of these tradeoffs. However, some broad guidelines for managerial processes can be obtained from a study of market dominance even when the specific objectives that firms try to achieve cannot be identified.

The rest of the chapter attempts to specify the efficiency of managerial processes that can be inferred from the specification of market dominance and market power in this study.

9.2. The Process

Note that the choice x of a non-price strategy affects the value V(x) as the consumer experiences it. This valuation, in its turn, determines the market share s(V) of the firm. In general, it can be presumed that each firm targets a subset of the differentiated products available on the market. Denote by v_j the market power of this subset of products over the consumers. This may, for instance, be measured by price cost margins. All the firms, that compete with the firm over even a smaller segment of this subset, will reduce its market share. Now, the firm uses non-price strategies to enable the consumers to identify the value of the products to them. Let a value x* reveal the valuation vx* and the corresponding market share s_j*. The market power of the firm with respect to this subset of products will then be $I_j = v_j\, s_j*$. Obviously I_i is the market power attributable to the chosen subset of products irrespective of the position of the specific firm w.r.to its rivals. In practice, firms may exceed s_j*. A realized market share s_j then indicates that the market power of the firm is

$$m_j = I_j s_j = v_j\, s_j*\, s_j$$

This can be inferred from the arguments of Landes and Posner (1981) noted in ch.2. In the previous chapter it was acknowledged that s_j* can be measured by market share and so on. Such choices may not maximize short term market power.

$$s_j* = s_j - \sum v_k\, s_k^2 / v_i s_i\, (n\text{-}1);\ \text{where the summation is over } k \neq j$$

Consequently, it can be inferred that

$$m_j = v_j s_j^2 - \sum v_k s_k^2 / (n - 1)$$

In the context of markets of this nature, competitive or efficient markets can be characterized by $s_i = s_i*$ for all i. In other words, every firm realizing the potential value of its products will not constitute anti-competitive behavior. It can be readily verified that under such conditions $m_j = 0$ for all j. For, $s_j = s_j*$ implies that $\sum* v_j\, s_j^2 = v_i\, s_i^2$, where $\sum*$ is summation over j = 1, 2, …, n. Consequently, $\sum v_j\, s_j^2 = (n\text{-}1) \sum* v_j\, s_j^2$. Hence, $m_j = 0$ for all j. (These conditions are too rigid. It can therefore be inferred that, in general, $m_i > 0$.) Let s_{ij} be the share of the characteristic i in the total of all non-price choices that it adopts. The market power of characteristic i of firm j can be defined as

$$m_{ij} = v_j\, s_{ij}^2 - \sum v_k\, s_{ik}^2 / (n\text{-}1)$$

The value of m_{ij} may then be used to infer the efficiency of the managerial choices and their effect on the market for the products of the firm. Note, however, that changing the position of the market demand is one aspect that the management is concerned about. The firm may also direct its management practices to ensure long run stability of its market dominance, market shares and so on. Such choices may not maximize short term market power. In practice, $s_j < s_j*$ and $m_j < 0$ occurs whenever the cost of implementing non-price choices (or the managerial incompetence and inefficiency in implementation) exceed the value generated in its interface with consumers.

9.3. The Inferences

First, observe that v_i may be high or low depending on the elasticity of demand. Similarly, s_i may be high or low since it is determined by the range and intensity of the product choices. Second, for both the product choices and non-price strategies the characterization of their influence may be on the market forces external to the firm or the organizational arrangements within the firm. It must also be acknowledged that several choices exist in each of these classifications. Clearly, the inferences for management practices will depend on the specific segment to which the choices belong.

Consider the most favorable context in which v_i as well as s_i are high. Clearly, the markets for its products are favorable and its strategies enable it to maintain and consolidate its market share. In the early stages of strategic management debate Porter (1980, 1985) pointed out that firms that have stable markets for their products should consolidate their position by ensuring that production and logistic aspects of management are robust. For instance, the firm may strengthen its supply chain management and take advantage of external market conditions. Production choices are not likely to change. Assume, on the other hand, that v_i is transient and fluctuating. This may correspond to new product introduction where the consumer cannot express loyalty. While it is reasonable to argue that the firm should concentrate on efficient production and distribution it may be far more important to adopt hit and run policies to take advantage of external market conditions to maximize short run profits. Maintaining high short un market shares may none the less be important. This is the theatre of market arenas that McGrath (2013) advocated. Maximization of market share is not, by itself, a goal. Non-price choices of such firms may be essentially to differentiate themselves from rivals.

Conceptually there may be situations in which v_i is high but s_i is low. At least initially it should be inferred that the demand for the products of the firm is low despite its garnering high price cost margins. The firm will then look inward to its competence and resources to examine the possibility of improving its non-price choices that can alter the market conditions relative to rival firms.

Somewhat differently there will be instances were v_i is low but s_i is high. The markets in which the firm is operating are highly competitive. Whether the firm will change its product line choice toward those that promise higher v_i will depend on the resources available and organizational efficiency. The possibility exists that the firm should choose non-price strategies to improve its markets since a low v_i may indicate that the consumers are not able to ascertain the value of the products. The choices available to the firm will mostly consist of external factors that should be improved.

The worst possible scenario is one where the v_i and s_i are low. Conceptually it may be difficult to alter the organizational arrangements significantly. Given its resources the firm may attempt new product lines that promise higher v_i values.

From an operational viewpoint the analysis should start with the priority that the firm assigns to its objectives and product and non-price strategies that provide it the observed market power. Such an analysis would indicate whether the firm is better prepared to pursue internal strength or would benefit by modifying or controlling features external to it. Clearly, whether the firm should pursue strategies based on internal strength or external market conditions will be determined by such a perusal. However, it should be obvious that the actions of the management will ultimately determine the direction in which a firm will orient itself.

9.4. Orientation of Strategies

The example that was pursued in earlier chapters provides an indication of how the analysis of managerial alternatives should proceed.

Observe that F_1 has a high MS but it is operating with a group of products where the price cost margins are low. In general, the low PCM may be due to a high elasticity of demand for its products and/or high costs of producing and selling its products. If it is the former the only option would be to move to a related product group where it will have greater control on prices. However, the firm is not pursuing this method probably due to certain inflexibility in the organizational arrangements. Instead, it depends on improving its managerial to production worker ratio so that it can reduce costs. In this sense the strategies of the firm are inward oriented.

F_2 is achieving high overall profits though its PCM and MS are at best modest. A defensive management prefers to maintain its profit position and utilize modest adjustments to its product and non-price strategies. There is no indication that it attempts improvement in MS or PCM since they may lead to a reduction in overall profits.

F_3 has the highest PCM but has a low MS. One of the reasons is obviously its pricing policies. There is no indication of a reassessment of pricing policy. Instead, it is adopting product and non-price strategies that will improve its market share and take control of external market conditions.

F_4 may be a relatively small firm. Its share prices are high indicating that in the view of individuals providing finances it has a good market potential. There is no indication of changing product or non-price choices to improve MS or PCM. (When a new innovative product is introduced in the market the firm depends on venture capital that provides the firm the necessary finances based on its valuation of the proposed business.)

F_5 has the highest market value in the group. That is, it has a strong base of capital assets and the market valuation is that it has good long run prospects. As of now, it appears that the management is very inefficient. Only a few product and non-price strategies to improve its existing product portfolio are discernible.

F_6 has a low PCM as well as MS. The management strategies are not indicating any product or other strategies to improve the PCM. Hence, they employ predominantly inward oriented strategies to maintain their MS.

In general, most firms in this sample adopt defensive and inward oriented strategies to protect what they achieved. Changing production strategies is rather expensive. Most of these firms are reluctant to make major strategic changes. At the most they are making adjustments that suit existing capital equipment and organizational capabilities rather than trying any drastic changes. There is little indication of strategies that are forward looking to improve their current state.

One important observation is the need to account for the range of objectives that any one firm is pursuing to identify its strategic orientation. Clearly, usable information can be obtained only by conducting an analysis of the changes in the attainment of objectives that strategic changes bring about. A more definitive notion of the orientation, inward or outward, of the strategies is also warranted.

9.5. Lessons Learnt

The market power measurement can only provide an indication of the nature of strategic changes that can improve the position of a firm. They can also suggest whether the product choices made by the firm improve their market position or assist the firm in rearranging their management practices. Similarly, though most non-price choices are expected to be outward oriented some of them will only improve their efficiency. The critical need is to ascertain the efficacy of strategies to enable consumers to identify the intrinsic value of the firm's products since it is not available in the characterization of market dominance or market power. In other words, an index of market power of each firm based exclusively on s_i^* can be constructed and used in this type of analysis. It is also clear that the changes in the objectives brought about by strategic choices need an assessment to complement the information contained in their market power.

CHAPTER 10

IN RETROSPECT

"Modern work demands knowledge transfer: the ability to apply knowledge to new situations and different domains. Our most fundamental thought processes have changed to accommodate increasing complexity and the need to derive new patterns rather than rely on familiar ones. Our conceptual classification schemes provide a scaffolding for connecting knowledge, making it accessible and flexible." - (Epstein, 2019, p.48).

Abstract

An overview of the role of non-price competition and its contribution to market power of different strategies of firms has been attempted. Many difficulties with the identification of non-price strategies relevant to specific industries and their measurement have been highlighted.

10.1. Non-Price Competition

There has been an increasing acknowledgment that non-price strategies adopted by firms provide them market dominance and market power resulting from them. Indeed, the idea that firms in an industry produce differentiating but substitutable products is testimony to such an acknowledgment. However, the recognition has been symbolic and anecdotal. In general, no serious attempts have been made to integrate them into a welfare theoretic framework. One reason for the neglect arises from the notion that they have an essential contribution to value increases that consumers experience and as a result regulation of any kind is not desirable. Similarly, there has been a contention that attempts to regulate such strategies will stifle innovation. These views have been prevalent contrary evidence notwithstanding.

One of the primary contributions of this study is in arguing that the gains to the consumer can be folded into a welfare theoretic analysis which will nevertheless show that there can be losses to the consumers depending on these non-price strategies. The fundamental basis of the argument is the balance between the value of the information content to the consumer (which can be justified up to a level of their use) versus the profit maximizing (or shareholder value maximizing) motivation that leads to an excess over welfare maximizing levels.

Previous studies relating to the market power of industries were at the aggregate level and considered the imperfection in the product markets as the only source of such distortion. As it turns out they did not make any attempt to acknowledge the role of the competitive capture of market shares by the rival firms in the market let alone measure their effects. This study developed the concept and measurement of market power at the firm level, as opposed to a macro level dealing with industries, and disaggregated the quantum of market power provided to each firm by specific non-price strategies. This approach adds to, and does not try to suggest replacement, of the market power due to market imperfection.

Since price determination is not the primary channel through which non-price strategies affect firm behavior it was necessary to show that market shares replace prices in the determination of market power. The Herfindahl indices were adopted as the basis of its measurement after accounting for the multidimensional nature of such strategies.

When such a measurement is available the natural question will be about the mechanism of taking note of the value increasing aspects of such choices. A theoretical argument is presented to prove that such effects can be captured by adequately modifying the market share of a firm. It was also shown that such an intuitively obvious extension of the Herfindahl index provides valuable information.

For all practical purposes, the implied conflict of interest between the consumers and the owners of the firm result in the necessity for regulation. Equally important was a demonstration that earlier notions of regulatory norms can be extended to include these modifications. The recognition that the lowest market share, which cannot be generalized to all firms and industries, forms a readily measurable basis provided the method of defining regulatory measures. Consider the level of market power of specific non-price choices. It was shown that there is an inverse relation between the market share of a non-price choice and the number of such strategies employed by a firm. This restores the conventional logic of regulatory measures.

It is therefore claimed that a significant theoretical basis has been made available to examine all the relevant consequences of non-price strategies of firms. The delineation of market dominance and market power, when combined with these developments, enables us to make significant progress. However, qualitative aspects of the infringements associated with such choices could not be brought into the fold of the analysis.

These results are very general, and not specific to the features of any one industry or a firm within it. Empirical work related to any one or more industries will necessitate emphasis on idiosyncrasies related to them. Some modification may be called for.

10.2. Identification of Strategies

A few observations about the non-price choices of firms are in order.

A universally acceptable set of strategies cannot be enunciated. The diversity of specification of non-price dimensions depends purely on the ingenuity of the management of firms. However, the search for differences across firms and industries may be worthwhile from the viewpoint of firms and regulatory policy. Note that some of the qualitative dimensions that require attention in the context of cyberspace and internet related products and services can also be quantified. A few attempts are currently under way. It is premature to evaluate them. The yardsticks regarding regulatory policy, that can be directed towards them, are also at best fragmentary. Further progress may be expected in the foreseeable future.

Given the multi-dimensional nature of non-price strategies it is necessary to look beyond Herfindahl indices to explore their effect on market power. Though Rao (2009, 2012) made several attempts there is still a necessity to provide a theoretically sound approach to their integration into welfare theoretic analysis. Empirical observation generally suggests that the Herfindahl index overestimates the industry level market power. This was also noted in the context of the Linda index. The other available measures do not appear to be superior. The search for an index, which can be applied at all levels, and yet have a theoretically justifiable relationship, need further analysis. The fact that quantification, and econometric methods generally, cannot be justified by utilizing any economic theory are well known. As of now it is imperative that this deficiency is acknowledged and the results using such practices are interpreted with caution.

Non-price strategies, even when firms can maintain some distinctiveness and superiority, can be imitated to reduce the market power of a firm. If two, or more, firms compete to gain superiority w.r.to the same strategies they can be easily discovered and imitated to reduce their market power. As a corollary, firms are likely to succeed in achieving superiority and market power if they maintain distinctive choices relative to others.

On the other hand, it would be more difficult to imitate product line choices in the rivals' endeavor to reduce the market power of a firm. Similarly, strategies that can provide goodwill of consumers, workers, input suppliers and marketing agents may be far more difficult to compete away since they are intangible and difficult to reduce once they have taken root.

Non-price strategies will be of use in creating goodwill in the initial stages when firms are attempting to improve their stock of goodwill. Similarly, achieving superiority w.r.to market shares may be easier than maintaining them at high levels over time. Therefore, it can be maintained that tracing market dominance over time and identifying strategies that contribute to such stability vs. those that can be easily competed away becomes essential from a medium-term point of view.

Yamin et al (1999) pointed out that a firm using a complex combination of two or more strategies to achieve market dominance tends to outperform those that adopt a single strategy. That is, a firm that essentially concentrates its efforts on a few strategies is more likely to be less successful compared to one that is more diversified. For, an easily identifiable non-price strategy can be easily imitated. This reduces the market power of the firm if such a choice is adopted in isolation. Some other strategy, used in tandem, may provide greater overall market power. Such methods were presented in earlier chapters.

On occasions, it was pointed out that certain past decisions of the firm may have contributed to the goodwill of consumers towards the firm. For example, the firm may have come to the rescue of local people experiencing a devastating flood or drought. This may contribute to or enhance the goodwill of consumers towards the firm. Similarly, it was pointed out that a firm, which feels that it cannot win over rivals by utilizing any competitive mechanism that it can think of, may resort to cheating, intimidating, or downright assault. They may also tacitly prevent competitors from getting supplies. Such instances, though not rare, are much harder to document on a case by case basis and bring them into the fold of reasoned analysis.

Something as complex and time varying as the strategic choice that provides a firm the market power it desires cannot be folded into a single theory just as the notion of generic strategies cannot account for the diverse circumstances of non-cooperative rivals in the market. Equally clear is the fact that no amount of case descriptions can offer insights into what the management and/or policy maker should do in a new situation. A pragmatic choice is essential to provide operationally feasible alternatives in specific contexts. As Levis (2009) put it,

> "incumbents have to cover an infinitely broader landscape: new opportunities are at best hazy and threats could be lurking anywhere. It is not just new technologies, new competitors and business models that could change everything, but so many things that don't seem to make sense." - (Levis, 2009, 329)

10.3. Looking Ahead

Profit maximization may not be the objective of all firms. Some firms may maximize market share. Others may find a large size of capital necessary. Yet others may view the goodwill of the consumers as paramount to their survival and growth. Clearly there is a likelihood that strategies to achieve goodwill of consumers will be different from those emphasizing profit. It has not been possible to establish a relationship between the different objectives of a firm and the contribution of non-price strategies toward each of them. Firms are likely to achieve their objectives if they concentrate on strategies that are suitable to their resource base and core competence. This is an area that needs further exploration.

Though it was possible to define firm level as well as strategy specific measures of market power decoding the relationship between them is quite complex. The mechanisms of how different non-price strategies of firms combine to generate the firm level market power needs further analysis. Similarly, the channels through which the interactions of rival firms determine the market power in the industry remain unexplored.

It is equally important to identify the nature and extent of the difference between consumers seeking maximum value for the products and the extent to which firms pursuing different objectives deliver them. Further progress to make such distinctions is necessary.

It is clearly understood that some non-price strategies, such as advertising, warranties, and many others, are subject to regulatory policy to eliminate or restrict the market power they offer firms. In other contexts, regulatory policy may inhibit innovation. A far more detailed, and perhaps a different kind of, analysis would be necessary. To that extent, the dis-aggregation suggested here, while it is an improvement over conventional studies, leaves many dimensions open for further analysis and debate.

In the final analysis, as Pinker (2018) put it,

> “the first attempts to quantify a concept are always crude, and even the best ones allow probabilistic rather than perfect understanding.” - (Pinker, 2018, 404)

In a wider context, the proof of useful work is its practical relevance. The tools chosen to approach the issues, no matter where they come from, should be efficient to answer the question. Somewhat broader working hypotheses and their implementation in practice are awaited. More imagination and freedom of mind in specifying new concepts, methods of measurement, and broader interpretations that benefit both the managers and public policy are necessary.

It can be concluded that despite significant progress in this study some aspects of the conceptualization as well as quantification require further refinement.

REFERENCES

Alleman, James, Baranes, Edmond, and Rappaport, Paul. 2019. "Multi-Sided Market and Platform Dominance". Accessed May 14,2020. http://hdl.handle.net/10419/205162

Baumol, William. "On the Theory of Oligopoly", *Economica*, Vol.25 (1958): 187-198.

Baumol, William. *Business Behavior: Value and Growth*. New York: McMillan.

Baumol, William. "Contestable Markets: An Uprising in the Theory of Industry Structure", *American Economic Review*, Vol.72 (1982): 1-15.

Beattie, Alan. 2009. *False Economy*. NewYork: Viking.

Boal, William. "Testing for Employer Monopsony in Turn-of-the Century Coal Mining", *Rand Journal of Economics,* Vol.26 (1995): 519 – 536.

Boal, William., and Ransom, Michael. "Monopsony in the Labor Market", *Journal of Economic Literature*, Vol.35 (1997): 86-112.

Bolton, Ruth., Gustafson, Andres., McColl-Kennedy, Janet., Sirianni, Nancy, and Tse, David. "Small Details that Make Big Differences: A Radical Approach to Consumption Experience as a Firm's Differentiating Strategy", *Journal of Service Management*, Vol. 25 (2014): 253-274.

Brander, James., and Zhang, Anming. "Dynamic Oligopoly Behavior in the Airlines Industry", *International Journal of Industrial Organization*, Vol.11 (1993): 407-435.

Cairns, Robert. "Reflections on the Lerner Index of Monopoly Power", *Review of Industrial Organization*, Vol.10 (1995): 83-96.

Chandler, Alfred, 1990. *Scale and Scope: The Dynamics of Industrial Capitalism*. Cambridge: Harvard University Press.

Christakis, Nicholas., and Fowler, James. 2009. *Connected*. Boston: Little, Brown and Company.

Classens, Stijin. 2009. "Competition in the Financial sector: Overview of Competition Process". Accessed March 11,2020. https://www.imf.org/xternal/pubs/ft/wp/2009/wp0945.pdf

Coates, Ken., and Morrison, Bill. 2016. *Dream Factories*. Toronto: Tap Books.

Conley, Chip. 2018. *Wisdom @ Work*. New York: Double Day.

Crilly, Donal. “Recasting Enterprise Strategy: Towards Stakeholder Research that Matters to General Managers”, *Journal of Management Studies*, Vol.50 (2014): 1427- 1447.

Cyert, Richard, and March, James. 1963. *Behavioral Theory of the Firm.* Engelwood Cliffs: Prentice Hall.

Dansby, Robert., and Willig, Robert. “Industry Performance Gradient Indices”, *American Economic Review*, Vol.69 (1979): 249-260.

Dixit, Avinash., and Norman, Victor. “Advertising and Welfare”, *Bell Journal of Economics*, Vol.9 (1978): 1-17.

Ellickson, Paul. “Supermarkets as a Natural Oligopoly”, *Economic Inquiry*, Vol.51 (2013): 1142-1184.

Elzinga, Kenneth., and Mills, David. “The Lerner Index of Monopoly Power: Origins and Uses”, *American Economic Review*, Vol.101 (2011): 558-564.

Epstein, David. 2019. *Range*. New York: River Bend.

Fischer, Thorsten., and Kamerschen, David. “Measuring Competition in the U.S. Airlines Industry Using the Rosse-Panzar Test and Cross-Sectional Regression Analysis”, *Journal of Applied Economics*, Vol.6 (2003a): 73-93.

Fischer, Thorsten., and Kamerschen, David. “Price Cost Margins in the U.S. Airline Industry Using a Conjectural Variation Approach”, *Journal of Transport Economics and Policy*, Vol.37 (2003b): 227-259.

Frei, Frances, and Morriss, Anne. 2012. *Uncommon Service*. Boston: Harvard University Press.

Gannet, Allen. 2018. *The Creative Curve.* New York: Crown Publishing Group.

Goldfeld, Stephen., and Quandt, Richard. “The Estimation of Structural Shifts by Switching Regressions”, *Annals of Economic and Social Measurement*, Vol.2 (1973): 475-485.

Gundlach, Gregory, and Moss, Dianna. “Non-Price Effects of Merger: Introduction and Overview”, *Antitrust Bulletin*, Vol.63 (2018): 155-168.

Gurley, John, and Shaw, Edward.1960. *Money in a Theory of Finance.* Washington, D.C.: Brookings Institution.

Hajivassiliou, Vassilis. 2019. “Switching Regressions with Imperfect Regime Classification Information: Theory and Applications”, accessed April 25,2020. http:/eprints.lse.ac.uk/103119

Heath, J. (2010*), Economics Without Illusions* (New York: Broadway Books).

Klusowski, Jason., Yang, Dana and Brinda, W. “Estimating the Coefficients of a Mixture of Two Linear Regressions by Expected Maximization”, *IEEE Transactions on Information Theory*, Vol.65 (2019): 315-3524.

Hall, G., and Hale, Rosemary. "Monopoly in Motion Dynamic Economics in Antitrust Enforcement", *Virginia Law Review*, Vol.41 (1955): 41-478.

Hall, Marshall, and Tideman, Nicholas. "Measures of Concentration", *Journal of the American Statistical Association*, Vol.62 (1967): 162-168.

Hall, Robert. "The Relation Between Price and Marginal Cost in U.S. Industry", *Journal of Political Economy*, Vol.96 (1998): 921-947.

Hall, Robert. 2018a. "New Evidence on the Markup of Prices over Marginal Costs and the Role of Mega Firms in the U.S. Economy", NBER Working Paper 24574. accessed January 14,2020. https://ssrn.com/abstract=3174506

Hall, Robert. 2018b. "Using Empirical Marginal Cost to Measure Market Power in the U.S. Economy", NBER Working Paper 25251. accessed on January 14,2020. https://ssn.cm/abstract= 3282951

Hanna, Leslie, and Kay, John.1977. *Concentration in Modern Industry: Theory and Measurement.* London: Macmillan.

Hausman, Jerry., and Sadak, Gregory. "Evaluating Market Power Using Competitive Benchmark Prices Rather than the Hirschman-Herfindahl Index", *Antitrust Law Journal*, Vol.74 (2007): 387-407.

Hausman, Jerry, Sadak, Gregory and Tardiff, Timothy. "Are Regulators Forward Looking? The Market Power of Copper vs. the Regulated Price of Mandatory Access to Unbundled Local Loops in Telecommunication Networks", *Federal Communications Law Journal*, Vol.61 (2009): 199-207.

Hayek, Friedrich. 1960. *The Constitution of Liberty: The Definitive Edition*. Chicago: Chicago University Press.

Hayek, Friedrich.1988. *The Fatal Conceit*. Chicago: Chicago University Press.

Harford, Tim. 2008. *The Logic of Life*. Toronto: Doubleday Canada.

Heath, Joseph. 2010. *Economics Without Illusions*. New York: Broadway Books.

Hernan, Vallejo. "A Generalized Index of Market Power", *Revisconomia del Rosaro*, Vol.4 (2007): 98 -108.

Hicks, John. "Annual Survey of Economic Theory: The Theory of Monopoly", *Econometrica*, Vol.3 (1935): 1-20.

Hurt, Karin, and Dye, David. 2016. Winning Well. New York: American Management International.

Keynes, John. 1936. *The General Theory of Employment, Interest, and Money*. London: Palgrave Macmillan.

Kiyota, Kozo., Nakajima, Takanobu and Nishimura, Kiyohiko. "Measurement of Market Power of Firms: The Japanese Case in the 1990s", *Industrial and Corporate Change*, Vol.18 (2009): 381-414.

Klette, Tor. "Market Power: Scale Economies and Productivity: Estimation from a Panel of Establishment Data", *Journal of Industrial Economics*, Vol.47 (1999): 451-476.

Knight, Frank. 1965. *Risk, Uncertainty and Profit*. NewYork: Harper Torch Books.

Koutsoyiannis, Anna. 1982. *Non-Price Decisions*. London: Macmillan.

Landes, William. and Posner, Richard. "Market Power in Antitrust Cases", *Harvard Law Review*, Vol.94 (1981): 937-996.

Larsen, Huric, and Fredborg, Jasper. "Strategies and Evaluating Strategies of Firms and Consumers" accessed March 20,2020. https//ssrn.com/abstract= 2507656

Lerner, Abba. "Concept of Monopoly and the Measurement of Monopoly Power", *Review of Economic Studies*, Vol.1 (1934): 157-175.

Lerner, Abba. 1944. *The Economics of Control: Principles of Welfare Economics*. New York: McMillan.

Levis, Kieran. 2009. *Winners and Losers*. London: Atlantic Books.

Liejesen, Mark. "Adjusting the Herfindahl Index for Close Substitutes: An Application to Pricing in Civil Aviation", *Transportation Research: Part E*, Vol.40 (2014): 123 – 134.

Linda, Remo. 1976. *Methodology of Concentration Analysis Applied to the Studies of Industries and Market.* Washington, D.C: Commission of European Communities.

Lubetzky, Daniel. 2015. *Do the KIND Thing*. New York: Ballentine Books.

Lutz, Bob. 2013. *Icons and Idiots*. New York: Penguin.

Marshall, Alfred. 1920. *Principles of Economics*. London: Macmillan.

McGrath, Rita. *2013. End of Competitive Advantage. Cambridge: Harvard Review Press.*

Mills, Alden. 2019. *Unstoppable Teams*. NewYork: Harper Collins.

Newman, John. "Antitrust and Digital Markets", *Vanderbilt Law Review*, Vol.72 (2019): 1497- 1561.

Parnell, Gregory. "Generic Strategies after Two Decades: A Reconceptualization of Competitive Strategy", *Management Decision*, Vol.44 (2006): 1139-1154.

Petruccelli, Joseph. "On the Consistency of Least Squares Estimator of a Threshold AR(1) Model", *Journal of Time Series Analysis*, 7 (1986): 269-278.

Pinker, Steven. 2018. *Enlightenment Now*. NewYork: Viking.

Porter, Jack. "Estimation in the Regression Discontinuity Model", accessed April 15,2020. pdfs.semanticscholar.org.

Porter, Michael. 1980. *Competitive Strategy*. New York: Free Press.

Porter, Michael. 1985. *Competitive Advantage*. New York: Free Press.

Posner, Richard. "Antitrust in the New Economy", *Antitrust Law Journal*, Vol.68 (2000): 925- 943.

Poundhouse, William. 1995. *Priceless.* NewYork: Hill and Wang.

Rao, T.V.S.R. 1989. *Economic Efficiency of the Organizational Decisions of the Firm*. Heidelberg: Springer Verlag.

Rao, T.V.S.R. "Multidimensional Herfindahl Indices and their Applications", *Journal of Quantitative Economics,* Vol.7 (2009): 37-47.

Rao, T.V.S.R. "Firm Specific Monopoly Power in Differentiated Oligopoly", *Journal of Quantitative Economics,* Vol.10 (2012), 85-97.

Rao, T.V.S.R. "Strategic Behavior of Firms in Differentiated Oligopoly", *Journal of Applied Behavioral Economics,* Vol. 4 (2015): 51-62.

Rao, T.V.S.R. "Objectives, Product Choice, Non-price Instruments and Firm Specific Dominance in Differentiated Oligopoly, *International Journal of Economics and Business Research,* Vol 14 (2017), 1-11.

Rao, T.V.S.R. and Rastogi, Ranjul. 1997. *Discretionary Managerial Behavior.* Dorderecht: Kluwer Academic Publishers.

Warren-Bolton, Frederick. "Implications of U.S. Experience with Horizontal Mergers and Takeovers for Canadian Competition Policy", in The Law and Economics of Competition Policy (eds.) Mathewson, Frank et al. (1990). Vancouver: The Fraser Institute.

Williamson, Oliver. "Corporate Finance and Corporate Governance", *Journal of Finance*, Vol.43 (1988): 567-591.

Williamson, Oliver.1996. *The Mechanisms of Governance*. New York: Oxford University Press.

Williamson, Oliver. "The Theory of the Firm as a Governance Structure: From Choice to Contract", *Journal of Economic Perspectives*, Vol.1 (2002): 171-195.

Yamin, Shahid., Gunasekaran, A. and Mavando, Felix. "Relationship Between Generic Strategies, Comparative Advantage and Organizational Performance: An Empirical Analysis", *Technovation*, Vol.9 (1999): 507-518.

Yannopoulous, Peter. "Defensive and Offensive Strategies for Market Success", *International Journal of Business and Social Science*, Vol.2 (2011): 1-12.

Young, Nora. 2012. *The Virtual Self.* Toronto: McClelland and Stewart.